Now What?

How a Gap Year of International Internships Prepared Me
for
College, Career, and Life

Monika Lutz

As seen in *USA Today, TIME, The Wall Street Journal,
Glamour,* and more!

***All of the events detailed in this book are real occurrences from my gap year of two years. Some events occur out of chronological order to reduce reader confusion. All perspectives are truthful representations of my own experience. Most individuals and companies have been renamed to emphasize that it is the experiences and lessons that are of value, not the labels.

ISBN 978-1-49221-801-2

Now What? is Dedicated to Those Who Have Supported Me from the Very Beginning:

Jared Polis

The Henderson Family

Andrew Abate

Anita Frank

Brian Scios

Chichi Natasha Wambebe

Chris Todd

Christopher Martinez

David Beaver

David Williams

Deborah Ohala-Bastres

Dr. Lynn Walker

Eric and Liz Swanson

Krishan Arora

Kurt Swann

Lynn Morgan

Matthew Piskorz

Lucas Siegel

Marcia and Jaime Lujan

Mario Morency

Michel Mein

Nancy Patch

Oliver Sohn

Probir Ghosh

Rodrigo Gonzalez

Sue Vernalis

The Kronenberg Family

The Sanchez Family

The Whitaker Family

Lark, David and Ben Corbeil-Crandall

And to Those Who Made Its Creation a Journey, not a Destination:

Team Lutz

Hassan Osman

John Ayroso

Ciara Corbeil

Bonito

Elise Delaware

Zhenghua "Z" Yang

Amy Humble

CONTENTS

Including topics of interest covered in the chapter

INTRODUCTION

Where the Story Begins

Seeing my eyes gaze back at me from the front page of *The Wall Street Journal* wasn't an experience I was accustomed to. I was squeezed in a hotel elevator when the woman reading over my shoulder asked, "Is that you, miss?"—which only made the experience more unusual. Truthfully I was honored, stunned actually. But underneath it all, I was puzzled. Why me?

When the year had begun, my New Year's resolution had been to get into Princeton, not *The Wall Street Journal*, *Time*, *USA Today*, or *Glamour*. Wasn't I just an eighteen-year-old from a town near Boulder, Colorado, who had left a pile of rejection letters behind to take a gap year?

Now, with my fifth national news feature printed in my hands, it was clear that my gap year between high school and college wasn't what had struck the nerve of the nation. Rather it was an underlying realization that tiger moms and trophies weren't making our kids happier, more academically inclined, or certain of their professional choices. There I was at the heart of it all—the Ivy League reject who had found all three, on her own homemade game plan. Perhaps I had found an answer.

That answer enabled me to live independently in six countries, gain valuable work experience through twelve highly competitive internships with leading international corporations and governments, earn college credit toward my degree, and often travel three days a week while staying within my own self-funded budget.

Ultimately my gap years enabled me to arrive at Harvard with two years of work experience, intermediate Mandarin Chinese skills, a full passport, life perspective, and firm decisions regarding my academic major and professional career.

To get to that point, I failed. Often. And slammed into obstacles. Everywhere. When that happened, I found myself asking, "Now what?"

The question "Now what?" was my guide in search of an approach to overcoming college apathy, career indecision, and academic idolatry after high school. Unfortunately the valuable gap year truths I learned from answering this question were sparse in the national news articles—even the ones I wrote myself—due to the slave master that is word limits. I yearned to tell readers the full story—of finding who I was and what I wanted personally, professionally, and academically—in the face of rejection, the death of a loved one, detainment, office politics, travel complications, safety threats, unemployment, lost spirituality, and loneliness.

I wanted to dispel pervasive gap year myths and illustrate that students *can* pursue their own paths and still get into their dream school. After all, while I was a trophy-cherishing, accomplishment-collecting, Ivy League–obsessed high school student, I was rejected from colleges across the board. It wasn't until after I took a year to separate myself from it all, to explore who I really was and what I really wanted for *me*, that Harvard became an option.

Before I left, my gap-year questions ranged from the general: "What does a gap year even look like?" "Can I afford a gap year?" "Can I stay in America instead of going abroad?"

To the academic: "If I take a gap year, will I ever go back to college?" "Won't the best schools look down on me?"

To the professional: "Aren't I too young to get prestigious internships?" "What will employers think of a gap year?" "Should I work, study, or travel?"

To the personal: "Will time abroad ruin my relationships?" "Won't I miss my friends and family too much?" "Are simultaneous travel, interning, and studying manageable?"

Before I left I craved personal answers to these questions from the eyes of someone who had lived it herself, but I couldn't find someone who fit the bill.

Until now. This is a raw, personal account of what I went through, what I learned, and where it got me so that students and their parents can have the first-person answers they deserve.

This is a gap year with a face—not a post-gap checklist. In place of to-do's, you'll find narration, dialogue, or an overview to portray the insights I hope to pass along. While I funded and organized my years by myself, readers interested in such a path should tailor their gap year with as many—or as few—destinations, internships, or classes as their personal and financial goals dictate.

I realize a gap year won't be everyone's answer to "Now what?" but if the defining moments of my story can inspire even a handful of students and their parents to pursue this alternative path, it would make opening my wounds and heart completely worthwhile.

CHAPTER ONE

April 1, 2010

Boulder, Colorado

Now what?

It's the question we ask ourselves when we've reached an end point.

When nothing seems to go as planned.

When the road ahead is undefined.

This is my journey of searching and discovering a fulfilling answer to the question "Now what?"

I come from a small, quirky town just outside Boulder, Colorado, where North Face jackets and closed-toed Crocs are considered business-casual attire. There my self-made parents sent me to a public high school where I sweated through my academic career inside a superficial castle built on golden trophies, wallpapered in ribbons and certificates, and cemented with awards. Abandoning folly and friendships, I crammed to maintain a superb GPA, run three clubs, and make it to my varsity athletic practices on time. Like tens of thousands of students from around the world every year, I told myself that getting into an Ivy League school would make it all worth it. And so the Ivy Leagues became my everything.

"Everything" was taken away from me with one word on April 1, 2010.

"No."

With this first e-mail, I only frowned. It was from Harvard. What was I expecting the committee to say? I clicked on the next e-mail with haste. Ever since I was old enough to spell "Ivy League," I had been waiting for this day—admissions decisions day. Up until today, I had created a world in which happiness and success could fit inside one large manila envelope. Where the number of awards I'd won, my test scores, and my executive titles could project my success rate in life.

Where a small committee's one-word answer could decide my future and worth.

The second time it stung. Wharton—no.

Yale—no.

Stanford—no.

Georgetown—no.

Boston College—no.

Pepperdine—not now.

By the ninth letter, the accumulation of that vicious two-letter word started to weigh on me. My throat tightened.

My mom, kneeling beside my desk chair, exchanged nervous glances with my dad. Simultaneously they placed their hands on my shoulders. I swallowed hard to suppress my tightening throat and scrolled to my final admission e-mail. The one decision I cared about most—Princeton.

No.

The butterflies in my stomach turned to gall. My entire body went numb.

Slowly I turned my bloodshot eyes—which were burning from my having taken three exams that day and my nightly habit of five hours of sleep—to my parents' disheartened faces. I held their gaze and summoned a quiet, stunned voice. "M-mom?" My voice quivered. "D-dad? Did I..." My voice broke off. "Did I just get rejected from college?"

I looked up as my eyes welled with tears and saw three walls around me plastered with awards, crowns, magazine features, and certificates. Their outlines blurred as my eyes struggled to restrain the tears.

I felt wronged! Where was my prize for sustaining a high school career akin to enduring a thousand paper cuts from one's own award certificates? I wanted to scream for a recount!

But I had no strength. I had dedicated the last four years of my life exclusively to reaching this moment. Ivy League acceptance was the epitome of "making it" in my world. It wasn't my parents' expectation; it was my own dream for myself. And I had failed. Still sobbing, I kept my head perfectly still, fixed on the screen. I couldn't look at my parents, who were still flanked on each side of me. I couldn't look at my cell phone, which flashed with inquiries from friends, counselors, teachers, coaches, and mentors. I couldn't look at my high school banner, which hung above my desk. I had failed each and every one of them.

"Now what?" I questioned the surrounding silence.

I faced two roads—go to the only school that had accepted me, a state school and my ninth choice, where all my accomplishments would earn me a seat in a class I'd already taken because I didn't apply to their honors program or advanced placement for my International Baccalaureate (IB) exams. *Why would I put in such effort?* I'd reasoned five months earlier as I clumsily tossed in my application. *My test scores guarantee automatic admission and I'll never* actually *go there. I'm basically doing this to please my counselor.* Locked in the lecture halls of that unwanted eighth-level backup school, I could spend the next four years drilling into my mind that I was never good enough for the Ivies anyway.

Or I could leave it all and forge my own path—take a gap year.

But what would I *do* on a gap year? How would I pay for it? What about college? What would future employers think about my having strayed off the beaten path? And what would my boyfriend, friends, and family think? I was peering over the cliff of where the paved path in my life had ended.

I looked back at the heap of rejection e-mails in my inbox.

I was going to take the road less traveled.

For the moment I didn't need an airtight plan. I just needed a distraction. I needed something that was exciting enough for me to divert all the questions I would get at school tomorrow and hold my head up high.

I decided on China. I'd traveled there a year before and heard about people working at orphanages or teaching English. Learning Mandarin in college seemed useful. Living there for a bit seemed like a good way to build up a foundation in the language.

Maybe this was a chance to explore my college major in real life before going to study it in school—"reverse education" seemed the best way to describe the approach. I could fill my year with internships, travel, and academic classes then reapply to college depending on which major and location I most enjoyed while abroad. I just didn't know how yet. *China is a good enough excuse for tomorrow*, I reasoned and went immediately to bed.

At school the next day, selling that approach to my classmates and teachers wasn't an easy task. Granted, I wasn't looking for their approval or permission. I just wanted to avoid the "Big College Question." Despite my attempts, however, my classmates were relentless. "You mean, you're dropping out of school?" or "What's a gap year?" or "OK, that's cool. But seriously, where'd you get in?"

It took all of my energy not to cry by the middle of second period. I couldn't believe how strangely people looked at me. When I said, "I'm taking time off to teach English in China for a gap year," they responded as if I'd told them I was quitting life. Like I was giving up. Like a gap year was an indicator of a student who had reached her peak and was on the way down. I was exhausted by having to prove that my gap year wasn't a year off to party my way across Europe, as so many people implied.

By the time I got home from school, I needed to take a walk. My parents and our Alaskan Malamute, Sonic, came along.

In the shadow of the Flatirons, I complained about Sonic's pace. "Seriously, Mom, Sonic's lagggggging. Can we please turn around early? The way I have to drag him, I feel like I'm weight training."

Sonic was a teddy bear at heart; I knew he'd rather watch me run than accompany me. He probably was trying to get out of our walk so he could return to his informal post at the edge of the open space where all the neighbors tousled his thick silver coat as they passed by. *He's probably just getting lazy*, I concluded. Granted, at 120 pounds and seven years old, Sonic had slowed down week by week.

"Why don't you take him home and get back to studying for your exams?" Mom smiled, poking fun at my obsessive studying habits. Now that I planned to reapply for college, my final exams and IB scores would be worth a lot.

Three hours of studying later, I needed another break. *Petting Sonic will relax me*, I thought, as I stretched and strolled outside toward my oversized puppy.

He lay about hundred feet away and didn't look up at me. *He must be napping again*, I thought with a chuckle. *He's always napping.*

I stopped laughing when I knelt next to him. He raised his eyes but nothing more.

"Hey, Sonic." I poked him playfully. "What's up, sleepy?" I ran my fingers over his head. His ears and skull were warm. I delicately touched his nose and paws so he would move, a game we used to play. His nose was wet, his paws dewy. But he didn't react to my touch.

"Sonic?" My voice was quiet now. His chest raised and lowered with harsh contrast. I gently pressed my head to his furry chest. His chest expanded then slowly decreased.

"Sonic," I whispered. "I'm here, boy." I wrapped my arms around him.

His chest expanded again—this time with a troubling force. Then slowly, slowly it decreased. Then it stopped.

I froze. I knew exactly what had happened. But I didn't know what to do. The pang in my stomach was the same feeling that stung me on April 1st. That pang that comes when you realize a part of your identity is gone. Slipped from you, like Sonic's breaths from between my arms.

In those arms was my eleventh birthday gift. In those arms was the puppy that had walked me to the bus every morning since fourth grade and had howled to welcome me home every afternoon.

Now that I was leaving on my gap year, I knew there would be no more taking the bus to school. For that I was solemnly glad, because after today I'd have to walk to the bus alone.

I stayed there, with Sonic in my arms, for a long time. With my eyes squeezed shut, I ran my fingers over his coat again and again. With each stroke a new memory with him played in my mind. I realized those were the sum total of memories I ever would have with him.

Before the month had passed, both my college dreams and childhood companion were gone.

*   *   *

Without Sonic or the Ivies, I had one final piece of my identity on the line—my annual high school awards ceremony.

Walking into the auditorium that night, I already had won the yearbook award for "Most Likely to be President [of the United States]," but tonight would unveil the most coveted prize, the Golden Apple Award. The honor was given to only thirteen seniors whom the faculty believed would make the greatest impact after graduation. Historically, the Head Girl (the student body co-president) won an Apple. I held that position, so I felt confident that tonight would change the direction of my current streak of disappointments.

They raised the curtain; thirteen chairs stood in a half-circle on stage. Our school's peppy college counselor began to read the list of award winners. One name. After another. After another. Until a single chair was left.

I sat on the edge of my seat, poised to stand. I felt the energy in the room, like a Miss America finalist who knows she's next in line for the crown.

"And the final name is..."

I imagined the emcee saying my name. I could hear her distinct Western accent rolling over the syllables. This was my night!

"Allison Loker!"

I stood up out of my seat and immediately shot back down. "Who?" I asked the person to my right.

She shook their head. "Never heard of her."

The auditorium clapped, but no one moved from the audience. "Allison? Are you here?" the emcee called out.

A group of students in the crowd yelled back, "No!" Apparently she hadn't even come.

My college dreams. My dog. And now my award. Gone.

The emcee continued to honor each student on the stage, but I didn't hear a single word. I couldn't take my eyes off that empty chair.

Someone tapped me on the shoulder from the row behind me. I was so focused that I didn't even flinch. The individual leaned in, startling me. I didn't recognize her. "That empty seat should have been yours, Monika," she whispered in my ear.

I shook my head lightly and whispered, "No, no. That seat doesn't belong to me." I stopped talking before my voice gave away the dam holding back my tears.

The moment the lights came on, I strolled out of the auditorium and climbed into the car. I watched the school building shrink into the distance. Then I burst into tears.

I felt forgotten. Utterly left behind. Like the bus named "On the Road to Success" had left my high school parking lot with all my closest friends and classmates and I didn't have a seat. I was the student body co-president, a varsity athlete, a team captain. I founded the business club, won the state mock trial award, was an executive for the National Honor Society— everything! I checked every box society had told me to check to get everything it said I should have. Now look at what was left— an empty mailbox and a barren trophy cabinet.

The empty chair on the stage floated in my mind all night. Truthfully I knew it wasn't a Golden Apple I wanted. I just wanted to know I'd made a difference. Underneath it all I was afraid I had become indistinguishable among the two thousand students who wandered those halls every day. It was the realization that even when I'd given everything I had, it wasn't enough for me to make the school's list of noteworthy students.

My college dreams. My dog. My awards. Gone.

I studied my teary reflection in the car window as I waited for a traffic light during the drive home. I barely recognized the girl who stared back at me. Who was I without all of these things? I needed to reconstruct my world from the foundation. I needed a gap year more than ever now.

After sulking into my room, I crawled under my bed covers. For the rest of the night, I had no notion of whether my eyes were open or closed. I couldn't see anything. I could only feel the lurching of my body as I tried to squeeze my eyes shut tighter. Tighter. I needed to know I was asleep, because I wasn't ready to face the reality of the past month. There had to be something else.

As the night crept on, I fell asleep for a few minutes, only to feel a rush of butterflies wash over me as I dreamed it was admissions day again. At the thought, I jolted awake to check the date. As soon as I did, I remembered that word—"no."

Back to bed. I dreamed I was running with Sonic, but he sat down to rest. I woke up and climbed out of bed to pet him. I stopped at my door when I realized he wasn't waiting at his gate.

Back to bed. I saw the empty Golden Apple chair floating on a stage before me. I jumped out of bed to rearrange my award shelves. "Gotta make space for it. Gotta make space," I mumbled groggily. When I managed to wipe the sleep out of my eyes, I realized there already was a space where the Golden Apple Award was supposed to fit. Now the hole irritated me. To me it was more than a hole. It was a crack and I had fallen through it.

I can't keep fighting the nightmares, I told myself. After scooping a sweatshirt off my bedpost, I went back to puzzling over a piece of scratch paper on my desk. I'd attempted to sketch out a list of places, dates, and possible internships for my gap year. The paper was still practically empty.

"Dream as big as you can, Monika," Dad had told me when we'd started to plan the week before. "Don't let anything constrain you. Just think about what would really excite you and write it down."

All I could think of writing was "San Francisco." A gap year didn't have to be entirely abroad, after all. I had a technology public relations internship already lined up there for the summer. I could extend that to fill some more time.

"Now what?" I asked the paper. "Where else do I want to go? What else do I want to do?"

Actually I had a lot of ideas about things I wanted to explore before I declared my major. I was interested in politics, fashion, marketing, economics, and China. Each interest was like a little puzzle piece. If I pursued them now, maybe I could discover how they all fit together and what the fresco of my life would look like before I had to make any big decisions about college, academic major, or career.

"Yeah," I puzzled in the cloak of darkness surrounding my desk. "Instead of going to college to learn and then hoping to apply that knowledge in the real world, why don't I go out into the world, discover what I want to do, then go to college and fill in the gaps? Instead of just *thinking* that I want to study something, why don't I go out and actually explore it in real life?"

That piece of scratch paper looked so empty, so intimidating. The entire next year was up to me. I had been in a structured school system for so long that I couldn't grasp that I'd been given a blank calendar and told to fill it with dreams. Whatever my year would or wouldn't become was determined by what I dreamed, planned, and earned. Suddenly twelve months looked very long.

Relax, Monika, you're just jotting down ideas. You don't have to commit right now, Dad's words rang in my ears.

He was right—I was just brainstorming, but that didn't stop me from feeling unprepared. I wanted to talk to someone who had been there, someone who had walked the path and ended up where they wanted to be! I couldn't find anyone. With no role models or examples to look to, I realized I'd have to make my future decisions based on my own predictions.

All right, Monika, I thought. Just start step by step. Where could I picture myself working and where was I qualified to go? Was I ready to go abroad for such a long period of time?

Looking up at the photo frame above my desk, I traced the smiling, sun-kissed faces of the French family I'd lived with two summers before in Versailles. I remembered the wafts of fresh baguettes in the mornings and the song of foreign tongues that could never be silenced. That summer I'd felt more alive than I had during all four years of high school combined. I was ready to live again! Yes, I was ready to live abroad.

With the French I knew, maybe I could work in Monaco. The marketing company I had interned for last summer had contacts there so I could ask them for an introduction. I scribbled down the company's name.

I'd have to change only one major component at a time. For instance if I had a marketing internship, my next step could be in public relations because the work was tangential. After having a high-fashion designer as a PR client, I could try to secure an internship on the in-house side with a fashion designer, et cetera.

I found out that the company I would intern for in San Francisco had a branch in London. If I performed well, maybe I could get a transfer there. From "San Francisco," I drew an arrow that led to the word "London." Just seeing the letters ignited a spark of excitement in my tummy, a sensation long muffled beneath exams and afterschool activities. *You're on the right track*, my heart seemed to be telling me.

My fatigue made it easier to be creative because I didn't have the clarity to deem any idea outlandish. Then I added, "China" and "India" in little thought bubbles on the side. Social entrepreneurship, creating companies with the intention to better the people served, positively impact the planet, and yield a profit, in India was firmly set in my mind. After all, at the beginning of the month, I never doubted that I would be a social entrepreneur after graduating from Princeton.

The sun peaked over the horizon, and I heard my dad typing on his laptop downstairs. The tapping echoed throughout the otherwise silent house.

Still in my pajamas and sweatshirt, I appeared in his doorway with the paper in my hands like a child on Christmas Eve waiting to talk with Santa. He glanced at it and smiled. Dad's support of my decision and knowledge of travel planning came from personal experience. Gap years are more common in Europe and since my dad is from Germany, he had taken a gap year to study karate in Hong Kong and explore a new culture after he graduated college.

He studied the progress I'd made—four thought bubbles and a couple arrows. "Good," he said. "Now that you've dreamed a bit, let's get realistic. What can you actually make happen and how will you pay for it?"

I crinkled my nose as if to say, *Are you really asking me the hard questions at six in the morning?*

He read my expression. "If you want Mom and me to let you delay school and call the shots, you're going to have to pay your way."

I nodded. That was exactly the way my parents had raised me. I saw how hard they worked to provide for my brother and me. I never could treat them as an extended line of credit.

"OK," I said with a sigh, realizing the early hour wasn't a worthy excuse in my father's eyes. "What are we talking?" I asked rhetorically. "I'll need core items: airline tickets, housing, food, and a few pieces of vital clothing, depending on the location. Airline tickets will be the most expensive, but they'll be easier to come by after the first few trips because I can accumulate mileage. I can fly from one city to another to reduce airfare and always fly on off-times of day, during off-times of the week, and off-season. Once I get to the developing countries, the price of living will be very inexpensive, so my budget will even out. I'll need paid internships and some scholarships too."

Fortunately I had accumulated a modest savings account during middle and high school by working as a lacrosse referee on weekends and babysitting. During my junior year of high school, I had worked as a supervisor at the local recreation center's "kids' night" every Friday. I watched dogs and houses over the summer and holidays. Moreover, I'm a saver. When everyone had new iPods and expensive speakers, I had a modest iPod Shuffle that I'd bought with my hard-earned money at age fifteen.

"Think of it this way," my dad said. "Start with a location or job you're interested in. Find out when the low season is so flights and accommodations will be cheap. Then secure the internship. Look for local or applicable scholarships. Start filing visas and looking for inexpensive housing at that point. Buy the tickets last but with enough time to get good prices."

I nodded. "Maybe I could get local businesses to sponsor my trip if I took pictures and created an art exhibit in their office upon my return? Also, friends and neighbors might sponsor me for certain countries to send them a postcard from the location and bring them back mementos such as scarves or spices from India or teapots from China."

I scribbled down these ideas and admired the paper. With only a few words, it still looked empty. Or maybe it was pristine, uncluttered by the external accomplishments that I previously thought would fill me up inside. Now as the darkness enclosed me, I had only my dreams to fill me up.

"Only when the jar is empty can the sky fill it up," a fable once told me. I was opening my future to the sky, to fate. I was breaking away from the incessant need to associate my worth with awards and honors. I simply needed a beginning point and a direction. The rest I would fill in along the way.

*   *   *

Eventually, with my rough outline in hand, I wandered into the kitchen for breakfast. My older brother, Norbert, was home from his state university for the weekend. He and Mom sat at the table, watching me cross the room. The only acceptance letter I had received—from my ninth-choice state school that granted automatic acceptance to students with my academic credentials—was on the counter.

Defiantly I dropped my gap year outline on top of it and opened the fridge.

Mom broke the silence. "You're being irrational, Monika. If you want to follow what God's telling you to do, you need to stop running away and listen. There's a reason for everything. Maybe God's plan for you is to stay in Colorado."

With my head still in the fridge, I glared at the door shelves.

Her words inflamed the exact point I was trying with all my might to disbelieve—that I wasn't actually Ivy League material. That I wasn't special or exemplary in any way because I wasn't good enough to go to any of the schools I wanted. That all the painstaking effort I had put into my high school career was worth exactly as much as that of another kid who had cruised through high school and was looking for a good party in college. I continued to scavenge the fridge drawers for food.

"Maybe you just need to realize that you push yourself too hard and you're actually more like these state school kids than you think," Mom told me.

I shut the fridge door and spun around. "No. I am not like them. I've worked too hard in my honors classes to take the same content as an entry-level freshman, the way they're going to make me. I can't go there!"

"Why don't you just give it a try, Monika? That's what I would do."

"Because if I do this..." I prodded the acceptance letter with my finger. "...I'll be living the life *you* want for me. But *I'm* the one who has to live with this choice, Mom. *I* will be the one spending orientation day counting the hours until graduation."

Norbert stepped in. "Monika, it's only four years. Just start in the fall, spend your summers interning anywhere you want, and you'll be done before you know it."

"Only four years?" My voice began to rise. "How long will four years feel if I spend every day focused on nothing else but 'getting done'? How long will four years feel when I have to scour my textbooks and lectures for the magic passage that tells me what I want to do with my life?"

Dad walked into the kitchen and stood on my side of the room. The manila envelope on the counter was tearing our family apart.

"That's how lots of people do it," Norbert replied.

I was still heated. "I don't want to go to college for the sake of it! Just because society, and you, and all my friends tell me to doesn't mean it's right for *me*." I batted the acceptance envelope away. "I need out. I need to see more than the squarest state in the Union before I know where I belong!" I paused, staring at my empty cereal bowl. "And...and maybe I'll come back, and I'll realize that this really is where I belong. But," I sighed, "don't you trust me enough to let me make my own life decisions?"

I wasn't looking for their answer. I put my empty bowl back in the cupboard and went upstairs. The envelope stayed on the counter.

Frustration had overtaken me—not with the situation but with myself. My family and community meant so much to me. Knowing they disapproved of my gap year made me feel torn and ungrateful. I wanted to please them. I wanted to respect them by following their advice. But I couldn't get over my own heart telling me that everything about following the beaten track—to attend a university where I didn't want to be, when I didn't even know what I wanted to study there—was wrong.

When I finally came out of my room, Mom was sitting in a chair near the top of the stairs. Her head was in her hands, but through her fingers, I saw that her face was white, speckled with tears. My stomach sank. Was this all because of me?

Tenderly I walked over and sat in the chair across from her, keeping my eyes on the floor out of guilt.

She raised her eyes and spoke in soft, teary words. "Monika, there are so many things in life that you can never pursue if you don't get a degree." She was interrupted by sniffles, "And...I...I just don't want my daughter's future to be limited. These...these obsessions with the Ivy League and varsity sports and student government—you created them yourself. Dad and I never told you to do any of it. We would love you just as much if you attended college here as we would if you were going to Harvard."

"But please," she continued softly, "please don't let these rejections ruin your future. If you don't go to college now, who knows if you ever will?"

My mom worked around the clock to support our family. All the while she always made time to drive me to school every morning, attend my sports games, and cook dinner every night. I wanted nothing more than to make her proud, as a way of thanking her for all the sacrifices she made for me. But to me, going to that ninth choice school would be settling for less, something my mom had taught me never to do.

"Mom..." My voice was tender now. "I *am* thankful for the way you raised me." I took a deep breath and tried to recuperate my voice. "I mean, you encouraged me to follow my dreams. You've given me everything. Now let me use what you taught me to make the decision *I* think is best." I closed my eyes to escape the image of her worry-torn face and said softly as I left the room, "I'll miss you in Nepal."

CHAPTER TWO

Life in the Jungle

Chitwan National Forest, Nepal

Nepal was no Monaco, but being in the developing world showed me that sometimes the most effective teachers are those you least expect.

"Did you know Nepal has the highest number of annual auto accidents on the entire continent of Asia?" Jeffrey, a member of my travel group, leaned over to continue reading his guidebook to me.

Nepal was a side-trip on my way to India. My travel group was a six-person, bare-bones, backpacker-style organized tour. The company coordinated hotels and transportation and provided a local leader to show us around. There were many student discounts and special offers, plus good ratings on travel advisory websites, so I thought it would be an affordable, safe way to explore Nepal.

Jeffrey prodded my shoulder with anxious anticipation to read me another factoid. Nearly thirty, he also was taking a year off but constantly spent time keeping up with his coworkers, calling his fiancée, paying bills online, and contacting his offspring. While observing him, I realized the value of pursuing a gap year after high school. Not only did I have far fewer restrictions, but I also had more post-gap opportunities available to me.

He rattled off another unnerving travel fact. I ignored him by pretending to listen to my battery-dead iPod. When he got suspicious, I even lip-sang to made-up songs.

"Wow, rabies incidences have shot up in this area over the past year," he continued. Highly educated, Jeffrey knew *all* the facts about every region we visited. What he didn't know was when to keep certain knowledge to himself.

Now was one of those times. Because right now, I was experiencing extreme motion sickness from being tossed inside our passenger van like a hot potato for the past three hours as we traversed twisting roads on the cliff-ledged sides of a mountain range in Nepal.

Even in the American adrenalin-addicted video-game market, this drive was too graphic and terrifying to exist as a game. The driver accelerated incessantly to fill every gap that opened in the road, regardless of proximity to oncoming traffic, monkeys, or the cliff ledge. Out of the corner of my eye, I already had counted three buses overturned on the side of the road.

I wished I were back in the United States where there are speed limits and safety regulations and standardized driving exams. I couldn't stop my mind from forecasting all the miserable outcomes that such a dangerous journey could produce. Who would know about me if something happened? I had purchased emergency medical airlift insurance before I left just in case, but would they even be able to find me in the back roads of the jungle? How much of a risk was I taking by being here?

Soon the terror ended, and we arrived safely to a series of huts in the thick of the jungle. I clamored out of the van and plopped down on the grass beside a stream to give my head a chance to stop spinning.

"Up! Up!" The tour guide extended his hand to me. "We've got to hike to our huts before the sun sets." With this command, Jeffrey began furiously flipping through his guidebook for an accompanying fact about post-sunset happenings. I sprang to my feet, denying him the opportunity to recite any findings that would leave me feeling more sick or afraid.

The next five hours led me over crocodile-infested waters, past rhinos in head-high grasses, and beneath bed-sized spider webs to a trickling riverbank. My shoulders pulsed from the weight of my backpack. I had tried to pack as lightly as possible: two quick-dry shirts, two zip-off pants, extra tennis shoes, some liquid laundry detergent, malaria pills, and a water-purifying wand. But after five hours, even carrying a twig felt onerous. I'd wrapped everything inside my pack in a black plastic trash bag and locked the different levels to deter thieves and raindrops.

Despite the literal weight on my shoulders, I felt strangely light. For as long as I could remember, I'd always had some athletic tryout or exam on the horizon that I had to worry about. Now time was a continuum of experiences, not a schedule of events. Without a doubt, if I had committed to a school by now, my mind would be wallowing in a cycle of endless to-do's, making this level of guilt-free lightness unattainable. With so many doors slammed in my face, I had nothing tying me to the person I was before. Every choice I made was for me, not college or grades. I felt...free!

As we neared another creek, five small village boys scattered from the water and ran into the surrounding grasses. I cautiously followed my tour guide and went into my hut for the night. Inside the air was thick with humidity. The only light came from stray sunrays peaking through the stick-lined walls. Beneath a cotton swath to the left were five wooden planks tied together. That was my bed. Weak from the trek, I couldn't care less. I slipped off my mud-soaked shoes and crawled onto the boards.

As I lay there, my ears rang with the buzzing of pests. The hum tormented me because I hadn't taken my malaria pills yet. My doctor confided that the pills would practically guarantee hallucinations. Cautious, I avoided taking them until I was in a desperate situation. Here in the jungle, I was too far away from a hospital to receive immediate medical treatment if a malaria-carrying mosquito bit me. On the other hand, I didn't want to endure hallucination-filled nights while isolated in a national forest two continents away from home. I entered a state of complete paranoia.

My senses went into overdrive. I could hear everything—a pounding bass of a heartbeat and a high-pitched ringing in my ears. Or was that the buzzing of a mosquito? Every couple of minutes, a sweat bead rippled down my skin. Jerking my body in response, I'd slap the sweaty region, terrified that it was a biting mosquito. I couldn't separate the two sensations.

Swat! *Oh. Just sweat.* Heartbeat. Heartbeat. Heartbeat. Swat! *That one, too. OK. I'm OK. Just think about home, Monika.* I started to count the number of meals, the hours, the seconds, the footsteps until I could leave the country. *One, two...*swat! Trying to sleep was pointless.

I climbed out of the tent to observe some giddy youngsters washing an elephant in the creek. The monstrous creature had the same personality as a puppy; he splashed around and sprayed his owner with water as he continued to frolic.

The children puzzled me. *Shouldn't they be studying or working or helping their families?* I thought. *They're wasting precious sunlight!*

As soon as I heard my thoughts, I realized how stuck I was in my past mindset of being an academic masochist. Back home I believed that working so painfully hard today would bring me bliss tomorrow. I thought the next day's moments would be sweeter if today's were extra bitter. In the end I didn't attain the result for which I had worked so hard.

So now what? Who was the smarter kid? I regretted the thousands of hours I spent in high school obsessing over everything college related. The perfect essay. The perfect test scores. The perfect résumé. Day in and day out, I saw the cost that my classmates and I paid for being "perfect": stress, loss of sleep, destroyed relationships—the list went on.

My eyes returned to the petite, smiling faces of the village boys. *What do these people care about?* I wondered. *Do they know what they are missing out on?* They may never learn the economic principles that explain why their cows cost one thousand rupees. They may never master the scientific background that would unveil why that same cow's milk must be pasteurized. Most likely their limited knowledge of history does not even explain who Louis Pasteur was.

Hmm, I wondered. *Maybe all those laborious advanced high school classes were a blessing, not a burden.* On one hand I mocked the pointlessness of my International Baccalaureate degree for its uselessness in the jungle, where individuals needed to know how to survive, not philosophize. On the other hand, I realized that such an advanced education was available only to those who were fortunate enough not just to survive but also to thrive.

What was a college education actually worth—both to me and to the world? I kicked the dirt patch next to me and frowned. I felt spoiled to be given an opportunity to go to any college at all—even if it was my ninth choice—only to leave it on the table.

Laughter filled the air as one boy's elephant sprayed the other like a two-thousand-pound water toy.

On the banks of that jungle river, I lost my urge to run away from home and escape my previous life. Suddenly I saw that education was a privilege. A rush of motivation poured over me. If I wanted to be better than who I was that day, education could be my ticket.

"Promise yourself now, Monika," I whispered to myself, "that whatever college you go to, you won't pass up the blessing of an education. Promise yourself now, Monika, that when you're cramming for finals and overwhelmed with academic work, you'll remember these people. Remember that you *have* to give your academics everything you've got because you got the chance!"

Maybe my time in Nepal should be about what I can learn from these people, I thought. These huts weren't just my new home; this jungle was my new classroom. I had been abroad for only a few short weeks, but clearing my head and seeing a new environment was already reshuffling my priorities. My attachment to what I thought I wanted to do professionally was about to crumble next.

CHAPTER THREE

A Change of Heart

Bengal Jungle, India

My expectations of India were unrealistic. I overlooked the possibility that the food might be too spicy. Or the 112-degree temperature would be too hot. Or the incessant staring would make me feel like I was being dissected in public. Some nights I had to stop myself from crying because I was dehydrated and couldn't spare the water loss. I'd never been so continuously uncomfortable in my life.

Facebook made me come here, I told myself, only half sarcastically. These days every school break seems to be a screaming opportunity for students to gallivant into dilapidated villages, hug the local children, and plaster Facebook with photographic proof of their journeys.

I got those pictures from working in the jungle. But before I could bring myself to post them, I wanted to describe in vivid detail what it actually felt like on the other side of the lens. That way maybe students could see beyond the glimmer of potential Facebook posts to the harsh demands of living there each day.

"Climb on." A young Indian entrepreneur motioned toward a wooden crate hitched to a rusting bicycle. That was our ride to the first village. I politely waited for him to hand me a helmet. He gave me a blank stare, wiped a trickle of sweat off his brow with the sleeve of his pressed white shirt, and again motioned toward the crate.

Oh, right, I'm not in America, I thought, and hoisted myself up.

America was a long way from where I was now—five hours outside of Kolkata, India, in the Bengal Jungle with two compassionate and enthusiastic entrepreneurs who were working to provide solar-powered lights to impoverished communities. They were on the website of the Unreasonable

Institute, an incubator for social entrepreneurs working on social and environmental problems, so I had contacted them via e-mail to find an opportunity to work with them on site. I stayed at their company's cement-clad compound while working there.

From my perspective, even when I was age sixteen, their work seemed exhilarating. As social entrepreneurs, they started businesses that would serve a triple bottom line of helping people, the planet, and yielding a profit. *My dad is an entrepreneur,* I reasoned, *and I look up to him. So why not be like my dad and help people in developing countries at the same time?* Before I even had my driver's license, I had made my decision; I wanted to be a Princeton Tiger and use my Ivy League education to create businesses that would serve more than the Board of Directors.

Two years later and with a rejection letter from Princeton in my hand, I decided to approach my education backward—work with social entrepreneurs now, figure out what I needed to learn, and then go study it.

The bicyclist started peddling. Squished behind me, the entrepreneur hollered, "The jungle here is beautiful but very dangerous. Tiger attacks take a lot of lives."

My eyes widened. I wanted to be a Princeton Tiger, not devoured by a real tiger.

If I hadn't been so focused on clinging to the crate, I would have guessed the number-one cause of death here was the heat. The temperature was more than a hundred degrees and humid. Sweat droplets clung to the cloth on my body, locking in the heat like a wetsuit I could never take off.

As a young woman, I had to wear pants and long-sleeve shirts. I had more pockets than an archeologist, and I checked each one incessantly to ensure no multilegged creature had nestled its way inside. The thought of all those creepy, crawly critters climbing their way through my pants made me wince.

As we rode deeper into the emerald vegetation, I inhaled "The Stench." Down certain paths, human excrement runs directly into makeshift sewage channels that frame both sides of the brick road. The sun bakes the mixture into an unforgettable odor. I suppose no one promised me that "taking time off to smell the roses" would actually smell good.

We peddled onward until the aroma of cooked fish drifted over the path. I grabbed my grumbling gut and hunched over a bit. There was very little I could actually eat. The water and veggies here weren't cooked long enough to be safe for my American stomach and the curries were too spicy. I was subsisting on mangos, stale crackers (most likely from the time when India was still a colony), and soda. I was constantly hungry and often lightheaded as a result.

To distract myself, I focused on the scenery. A mud-hut village seemed to grow out of the jungle. Massive tree roots clung to the two-room houses like ivy, leaving no spot untouched by their woody fingers.

From every corner leaked throngs of villagers who sprinted behind our bicycle or jumped onto our laps. Breathtakingly beautiful, the youngsters had hazel eyes juxtaposed by mocha skin and opalescent smiles. They owned no shoes but snapped pictures of me on their camera phones from a foot away.

Their genuine excitement to see, "an American!" puzzled me. Couldn't they tell that I was an award-losing college reject? Who would take pictures of that?

Click. Click. They continued incessantly. *Wait a minute,* I thought. *These people care more about eating tonight than how many points I got on the SAT. Maybe I'm worth more than my weight in trophies.*

*   *   *

The rushing crowds continued daily as we traveled with our main products, mini solar panels and lights, to hold town hall-like meetings with the village elders.

In the meetings, our local translators communicated for the entrepreneurs while I stood by holding the products, giving demonstrations, or smiling. As if being a foreigner added some legitimacy to the technology, just my presence guaranteed a turnout at our meetings. "Look!" My attendance seemed to shout, "White girls like solar power, so you should too!"

When scholars or government officials came through the villages, I discussed the products with them in English. Mostly I worked with the entrepreneurs to learn about their business models and concerns as they varied from community to community.

Each night I maneuvered through hordes of crickets fleeing from my presence as I walked to my sleeping cell. Their combined movements made it look as if I was wading through sprinklers, with little droplets spraying each and every way. But the crickets became old news fast.

At night croaking frogs perched so close to my sleeping-bag-covered legs that I felt the reverberations of their songs on my calves. That made me nervous. Actually their presence was only disturbing by association—if a frog was present that meant its dinner was nearby. Unfortunately for me, these frogs settled for nothing less than plum-size spiders. It was a symphony of sickness, really, and became my nightly dilemma. *If I scare the frogs away*, I thought, *the spiders will come. If I keep the frogs here, I'll have to endure the incessant auditory reminder that I'm a member of the food chain.*

"Please, Mr. Frog," I begged, "just do your job well."

Eager to leave the sleeping bag and my nightly worries behind, I awoke early every day to commence our tour du jour.

As we traveled, I watched women toil over 1930s-era pots perched over wood fires. Men pulled their oxen through the fields. Boys played soccer until the ball vanished into the night's inky cloak.

Where are the textbooks? I wondered. *Where are the standardized tests? Where are the rigorous schedules?* I couldn't understand what motivated these people. I was dying to ask the translators how the villagers could be happy without artificially created, self-imposed stress. I *lived* on stress in high school. Where was the drive and motivation? I wanted to know.

The answer was right in front of me. They didn't need schedules to motivate them. Hunger did that. They didn't need awards or prizes. Everyone knew one another's strengths and weaknesses.

Everyone here smiled and seemed to have a sense of purpose and value to add to the village. I hadn't found that for myself yet. So why were they listening to *my* advice to advance their villages?

The realization weighed on me throughout the week until our work brought us to an emerald pool of stagnant swamp water. The crowds and camera phones started to come out, as usual, as I prepared for the demos.

Here I am, I thought, *living the outcome I wanted to study at Princeton, and it's....nothing like I thought it would be. In fact it's nothing less than exhausting. I can't communicate with any of the villagers. I'm starving. It's bloody hot. I'm losing sleep for fear that an animal will snuggle with me in the night...*

The village elder started to speak. "They don't want electricity to run their stoves," the translator said. "They want to power their TVs so they can watch soccer."

I let out a puzzled laugh. The situation was unbelievable to me; I'd spent the last four years slaving through advanced schooling so I could go to college, graduate, and do exactly what I was doing now. And yet these people didn't want what I had to offer. They wanted live-cast soccer games!

Our translator kept talking, but my mind was somewhere else. As I stood perched on the side of the swamp, a feeling of frustration overcame me. Even if I *had* gotten into Princeton for my ability to cram and regurgitate, where was my competency score for positively impacting my community?

As I fumed internally, my eyes exchanged glances with a young girl in ragged clothing staring back at me. Even if I could speak her language, what made me think I'd have anything to say that was worth her hearing? I felt arrogant and embarrassed.

She looked down to brush a cockroach away from her knee. My stomach growled. A bead of sweat ran down my spine.

That was enough. *I don't have what it takes to endure these challenges day in and day out*, I thought. How dumb was I to think I could know the right career and major for me by simply liking the idea of it?

My gap year was supposed to be about learning by doing, not by reading textbooks. Fittingly this working experience in India taught me that I could confidently check "social entrepreneur" off my career list. *There's four grueling years at Princeton, $200,000, and a career dedication back in my pocket already*, I thought. In just twenty-one days, my gap year was paying off.

CHAPTER FOUR

Grow up...Faster!

San Francisco

Although it was my third professional internship, the eight weeks I spent in San Francisco gave me a crash course in professionalism and office politics unlike any I had experienced before.

"Well, it was great to speak with you, Monika. We're very interested in having you intern for us. Please check back when you're a junior...in college." The human resources director for one of the nation's top green technology and healthcare communications firms hung up the phone. It was mid-February of my senior year of high school, and I had used my previous internship experience at a prestigious New York marketing firm as leverage to prove that I was worthy of a simple interview. Well, I got a phone interview, but nothing else.

"Age again, Dad!" I had groaned, as I stood there hanging my head inside the car window. "When will it ever be about meritocracy? Why does my number of days on Earth make me more qualified to work for a company?"

He laughed then said, "Jump in." We pulled out of my high school parking lot, vacated hours before by classmates not constrained by my exhausting after-school activity schedule, and headed toward the house. "Sounds like you're going to have to prove to them that you can break the status quo. What's your plan?"

I smiled. My high school sweetheart Gordon went to college in San Francisco. If I flew out there, not only would it illustrate to the communications company how seriously I wanted to work for them, but also I would get to see my boyfriend again! That was a win-win in my eyes. I proposed an on-site visit to the company the next day.

Two weeks later I was on a flight to San Francisco for an in-person interview.

Leading up to that day, I completely submersed myself in preparations. My desk was covered in the company's press releases, recent company news, client news, and notes on their competitors. I researched my interviewers: their project accounts, school background, and specialties so that I could control the start of the interview by asking, "Judging by your background in X, why did you choose to work here?" This instantly would convey that I had done my homework and was thoughtfully considering the internship opportunity. After I heard their responses, I could delicately add what most interested me, showing that I had a distinct reason for why I wanted to work for *them*, not just *any* communications firm.

My next question would be, "Will you tell me about the best intern you've had? What were they like and what did they do?" I could then discuss how I fit that description and, if I got the internship, how I could display those qualities on the job.

I put my hand on my tummy as I peered out the humming airplane window. I could practically feel the butterfly wings flapping beneath my abs. I'd never flown anywhere for an interview before. If Gordon hadn't lived in San Francisco, I wouldn't have had the courage to travel there alone. The truth was, one final interview would decide whether I would ever be back.

*   *   *

"Mr. Simmons! It's a pleasure to meet you!" I extended a firm handshake to the young but distinguished interviewer. My blonde locks were tied back into a bun just above my black-on-black interview suit. The formality of my attire stood in stark contrast to the casual, techy office environment. Before flying out, I had scoured Banana Republic and Anne Taylor to find the perfect interview outfit. I chose to err on the side of conservative in my clothing to show respect for the company, even if all their employees wore jeans.

I sat up straight in my chair and coolly started off just as I had planned. "Before we begin, if you don't mind telling me, how different is your work here compared to your experience in the London office?"

He cut me no slack. "We'll get to that. Why are you here?"

The rest of the interview went back and forth like a game of verbal ping-pong. Each next question was a direct hit, leaving no room for me to pick up cues as to how I could articulate my experience in a manner that would be most interesting to him.

Finally he broke the volley and flatly demanded, "Look, Monika. I just interviewed two Berkeley students for this spot. Why would I ever give it to a high schooler from Colorado?"

Finally! A question I had directly prepared for! "Mr. Simmons," I said, "consider looking beyond my age and instead focus on what I've accomplished that will add value to your team. I have internship experience in a related area—marketing—and have exhibited leadership in your field by starting a green recycling campaign at my school and garnering the support of hundreds of students to participate. Further, what sets me apart is that you won't have to remold me—I come with no preconceptions of the communications industry. I'm hungry to learn. I have a lot of energy. And I'll dedicate it all to the job."

I closed my mouth and maintained eye contact. That was the end of my script. If that didn't win him over, I wouldn't either. Forty-nine minutes of questions and answers had passed. Mr. Simmons looked me straight in the eyes. His irises were a steely shade of blue with flicks of gray. The room was silent.

He blinked. "You just beat Berkeley. We'll see you in June."

*　　*　　*

Going into that final in-person interview, I'd thought earning the internship offer would be my greatest hurdle. It wasn't. Once I actually started work, the office seemed to divide into three camps: those who didn't realize I was so young, those who thought I was too young to be helpful, and those who thought my being so young meant that I was special and therefore a threat.

The first group treated me like a regular new hire. The second, despite being well paid and staffed on important accounts, thought I was "just a kid." Even though everyone knew I was eighteen, I had to act like I was twenty-five. My humorous references to homework, free periods, and GPAs were awkward here. In this adult world, being an executive of three of the most powerful student organizations on campus was like being the queen bee in an anthill. The game had changed. And I needed to figure out how to play if I wanted to make an impact and achieve the next step in my gap year plan: a transfer to the London office.

I began a search for where I could add value. How could I gain the trust of my colleagues?

I started with work ethic. Maybe if I outworked them they would value me. Within the first week, my chance to shine arrived. Melissa needed hundreds of journalist goodie bags stuffed, boxed, and mailed by hand. I jumped at the opportunity to help and worked all through lunch. Two other interns joined me for a little, but by the third hour, I was packing alone.

Excellent! I thought. *Surely I'll win points for being so tirelessly dedicated while the others bailed.*

When I finished the project, no one mentioned anything except Melissa. "Wow, Monika," she said. "You're so fast! You can do next week's fifty as well!"

Not exactly the thank-you I was expecting.

Darn it. I had just made myself the go-to goodie-bag maker. As I walked back to my desk, I made a mental note to myself: 1) self-sacrifice will go unnoticed; 2) don't become skilled at anything you don't like doing because you'll only get more of it. I was discovering the unwritten rules of corporate finesse.

That was only the beginning. The third group taught me more than the first two combined. One of my colleagues, Emily, unofficially led them. She didn't make eye contact with me when I greeted her. She frequently "forgot" to patch me in on team conference calls. And the harder I tried to be of value, the more Emily distanced herself from me.

"All right, Monika," my casually cool boss, Oliver, began during a team meeting, "we need an Excel sheet like this filled with this type of content for our client, Ellison, by Monday. Do you understand what an important impact your best delivery on this project will make?"

I nodded. "Yes, sir."

"Good. One more thing: I want you to check the news for these six search terms every hour until something breaks. As soon as it does, I need you to write an overview for the team and send it out immediately. Understand?"

I thanked Oliver for the project and rushed to my desk to get started. I had never done anything like this before, so I wanted as much time as possible to get the hang of it and deliver a quality job.

On day five of the seven-day assignment, an e-mail came to the team from Emily.

Hello, Oliver. Please find the completed Excel document for Ellison attached, in advance of its Monday due date.

Was this the project Oliver had asked me to do? I opened the attachment and raised my eyebrows in disbelief. Bingo.

Emily had done these types of projects before I started working there, so she had a clear advantage. But would she seriously scoop my work? Unsure how to respond, I focused on other projects.

The next day at nine in the morning, I checked the search terms Oliver had given me. Nothing came up. I tried again at ten. Eleven. Noon. Nothing. I ate lunch at my desk to monitor the search terms and finish another project. Nothing. Checked at one. Then two. Still nothing.

At 2:07 p.m., my colleague Sandra called me to her office to explain another project she needed finished. I rushed over with a notepad.

As Sandra briefed me, an e-mail alert from Emily popped up on her desktop.

Team: Attached, please find the press release for the news conference that just occurred in Ellison's industry. A brief is below.

My eyes bulged in disbelief. I had been checking for that exact release *every hour* and *twelve minutes* after I just checked, while I was in the middle of getting another project for the same team, Emily scooped the assignment.

"Monika," Sandra said as she turned to me, "weren't you working on patrolling relevant news coverage this week?"

How could I possibly answer that question without ranting about how totally blown away I was that Emily would do my projects behind my back? That fact wouldn't make any difference now.

I looked down at my notepad and replied, "Uh, yes, Oliver did assign that to me. But now that our team has what we need to move on, I'll dedicate all my focus to this new project you've given me. Thank you." I forced a smile and darted back to my desk.

I was completely confused. Here I was, trying so hard to prove that I was good enough for the team to trust me with more responsibility. Instead Emily misinterpreted my young age and eagerness as a threat to her job, competence, or position on the team.

If I didn't solve this problem, Oliver would think I simply wasn't capable or attentive enough to get my work done. Now what? I needed a new strategy.

*　　*　　*

On Monday, I met Emily at her desk and invited her out to lunch. Not surprisingly, she replied without taking her eyes off the computer screen. "I don't leave my desk for lunch. It's too time consuming."

I wasn't giving up that easily. "Well, I'd really appreciate the opportunity to hear how you got into the industry. I've seen what great work you do and how highly Oliver thinks of you."

In all honesty, I didn't *just* want to hear about her experience. Mostly I needed her to see that I wasn't a threat. I wanted to show her through my actions that I wasn't intending on outshining her; I just wanted to learn. Teams don't function when everyone is trying to protect their back from being stabbed.

"Fine. Make this fast."

I nodded as we power walked to a nearby restaurant. I had to set the tone fast: I was interested in learning, not competing. "Thanks for coming, Emily. I'll admit, I feel so many leagues behind you that sometimes I don't feel worthy of your time. Can I ask you about how you got so good at PR?"

None of my questions were specifically related to our projects. My overall goal was simply to convey that I saw her as an expert with a lot to teach me.

When we got back, she pulled a folder off her desk and handed it to me. "Here," she said. "It would really help the team if you could run this project. I trust you. Go ahead and take it."

I beamed. The situation with Emily made me realize the delicate world of communications that couldn't be learned at college—the soft skills. After that I made an effort to go to coffee every week with another colleague. As in Emily's situation, once I showed them how much I genuinely respected them and wanted to learn, they seemed to take me under their wings.

Maybe I'd found the benefit of being so young—as long as I proved that I was worthy of their time, everyone wanted to help me, teach me, and invest in me. The office soon became a hub of mentors.

At the end of the day, I headed home to a modest, hostel-like residence club just a few blocks from where I attended evening Chinese classes. During my search for an affordable place to live, I was afraid I wouldn't be able to find anything safe, reasonably close to work, and comfortable. Located on the brink of Japantown and Pacific Heights for approximately $1,300 a month, this place surprisingly fit all of those requirements.

"Night, guys." I waved to my colleagues and checked Facebook on my phone as I walked outside. My newsfeed was plastered with updates from former classmates. The GPA jokes, "#death-by-midterms" tags, and sorority puns ran rampant. The party pictures and self-shot Instagram photos followed close behind. I reached the bus stop. In the evening fog, the surrounding buildings were transformed into a series of haunted columns that oozed clouds.

The reality of the moment hit me—here I was in San Francisco. Educating myself professionally. Learning Mandarin after work for fun. Paying my own rent. My briefcase was filled with personal finance and money-management articles now that I had a real paycheck. I even opened a free Mint.com account to track my budgets and spending every month and monitor my trends over time. Meanwhile my former classmates were leading completely different lives.

In my fitted navy pencil skirt and button-down blouse, I felt grown up. Nonetheless my classmates still had something I wanted—college acceptance. The layers of professionalism I had acquired over the weeks couldn't untangle the fear of my unknown academic future that lurked beneath the surface. I exhaled into the evening fog, but the road remained unclear.

CHAPTER FIVE

Swimology

Yosemite National Park

"Take eleven days off just to *sit*? You're joking." Perhaps my first response to Dad's recommendation that I go to a meditation retreat was a little harsh.

"Seriously, Monika. I think it would be good for you," he replied, unfazed by my sass. "You said your gap year was all about 'learning life habits' and 'discovering more about yourself,' didn't you? If you really believe that, prove it."

I sighed. He was right. Meditation seemed like a good life skill to learn. Besides, if I thought I was too busy during a gap year, when would I ever have time?

The meditation clinic forbade speaking, using electronics, reading, exercising, eating meat, and writing. I roomed with thirteen other women in a one-story trailer divided by cloth sheets that hung from the ceiling. We slept in sleeping bags, shared two cold-water showers, three sinks, and a plastic front door. Among my approved possessions were three cotton T-shirts, two pairs of sweatpants, a bar of unscented soap, and a flashlight.

I slipped into my sleeping bag on the first night, filled with curiosity about how the next week and a half would impact me. I couldn't have predicted how I would learn that spiritual and mental wellness should not be foregone in the midst of academic and professional growth.

*   *   *

At 4:00 a.m. the morning gong bellowed, initiating an eerie predawn ritual. Electric lanterns were snatched and loose clothing pulled on. Women trickled into the hovering darkness of Yosemite National Park. Our sleepy saunter toward the meditation hall resembled a march of phantoms through a Halloween graveyard. With no natural light in the thick morning gloom, bobbing lanterns appeared to levitate along the dirt paths.

Once we arrived in the meditation hall, the instructor stressed the requirement to practice meditation, not just study it. *Hey, this is right up my alley*, I thought, and happily listened.

The teacher recited the following parable.

A very scholarly young man and an uneducated old man were sailing together. On the first day of the journey, the old man approached the scholar.

Old man: Young professor, please teach me something.

Young man: All right. Have you learned meteorology, the study of the weather?

Old man: No, professor. I have no education. I know nothing of meteorology.

Young man: No knowledge of meteorology? You have wasted a third of your life!

The old man went away very sad. The next day the old man returned to the young man.

Old man: Professor, please teach me something.

Young man: Well, have you learned geology, the study of the earth?

Old man: No, sir. I have no formal education.

Young man: No knowledge of geology? You have wasted two-thirds of your life!

On the third day, the old man returned to the professor, this time with passion in his voice.

Old man: Young professor! Have you learned swimology, the study of swimming?

Young man: Swimology? Well, yes...I am very familiar with the concept, but I have never gone for a swim.

Old man: You have wasted your entire life! The boat is sinking!

I smiled at the similarity between the instructor's parable and my gap year's "reverse education" approach to school, life, and career. Knowing the instructor approved of my gap year made me somehow more open to his teaching methods.

Nonetheless his next teaching was a much tougher sell. Vipassana meditation requires focusing on the breath and being aware of sensation. At 4:00 a.m. in a stuffy, dimly lit meditation hall, this was a tall order. I struggled to sit completely still on my garden mat for two hours. My legs ached, and my lower back felt strained from exhaustion. How could sitting still hurt so much?

In the silence I had nothing else to do but ponder my trajectory and motivations in life. Emotions bubbled to the surface of my conscientiousness like a kicked bottle of Coca-Cola. The meditation transformed my mind into a movie screen of film reels from all the repressed memories of my past.

During one session, I suddenly heard the voice from a sophomore-year phone call. *A car crash, Monika,* it said.

No! Not Jenny, not my team captain! I remembered my voice pleading in response. I mouthed the words as they echoed in my skull.

Minutes later childhood nightmares raised goose bumps on my legs as I helplessly reexperienced the time I had crashed my bike two years before. Even when I opened my eyes, the tingle still rippled down my spine.

The more I tried to clear my mind, the more vividly the memories flashed and then vanished entirely.

There was a single incomplete memory—April 1. I saw the e-mails again. I saw the orange ribbon in my hair. I remembered everything about the moment. But the sounds, the emotions were gone. All the disappointment, rage, and dishonor I felt so vividly that day was strangely missing.

Every day I wandered the dirt and desert grounds of the meditation camp, questioning why that most painful moment was unlike any of the rest. It wasn't until months later that I found the answer.

Back in the meditation hall, I learned that Vipassana teaches students to be mindful of sensation and approach every feeling with the awareness that it will soon pass. Learning to practice that awareness scared me, because in order to separate myself from pain, I had to be in pain in the first place. *That doesn't sound very productive*, I told myself. *I'd rather ignore problems and just submerse myself in distracting work until the problem goes away.* That was my usual approach to solving personal problems.

I tried the same approach at the retreat, struggling to avoid the flashbacks and uncomfortable sitting sessions. So I looked for distractions: counting gongs. Power-walking just below running speed. Sleeping during lunch.

My attempts lasted a day. Here I was, stranded in the middle of Yosemite National Park. The only person I was cheating was myself. The retreat was a pay-as-you-please event, but it was rude of me to waste the instructor's time by immaturely rebelling.

Hmm, I reasoned. *Discovering a method to overcome pain and suffering seems like a worthwhile pursuit. Maybe I should intensify my focus.*

One night I entered the meditation session with writhing stomach pains. We were only allowed two small vegetarian meals a day, an arrangement my stomach hadn't agreed to. It sounded the war chant. "Hungry!" it growled from my gut. "Feed me!"

I wanted relief from the shooting pain so badly that I focused all my attention on observing the sensations. Remarkably, when the bell rang to retire, the pain was gone. In its place, I felt refreshed!

The camp was teaching me a new approach to "letting go," of separating myself from suffering. Pain, as I learned, is guaranteed in life. Suffering is our interpretation of pain. In that case all suffering is optional. Why would I ever elect to have suffering in my life again?

I spent the following days relearning that lesson. On the last day, going back to regular life was awkward. Even when we were allowed to talk, I found I didn't have much to say. Most things just didn't seem important enough to tell others. Why mention the weather? They were outside too. What was so interesting about lunch? They had the same tofu I did. I realized how much time I'd spent "filling" space—in conversations in my mind with unnecessary worries, in my day with insignificant tasks. I was afraid to have free time, the meditation taught me. I was afraid to open my life to chance and release control to the universe.

I went back to the trailer to pack my sleeping bag, reflecting on the week as I did so. Before the retreat, I thought academic and physical performance was all that mattered. If I wasn't sick and had good grades, I should keep up the good work. Emotional wellness was very low on my priority list. Only sick people needed "mental health days," I thought.

Coming to the retreat, I knew I was suppressing my frustrations and pain. I cried over Sonic, college, and my awards for one day, then promptly distracted myself from the hurt with something else. Meditation brought all the pain and suffering back to the forefront of my mind.

But now, in practicing awareness, I had found a way to cope with the stress and rejection in my life. I couldn't prevent pain from occurring in my future, but now I'd be able to prevent myself from suffering because of it.

My sleeping-bag zipper hummed to a close. With the thump of a door, I situated myself in the car. The winds of changed whispered their welcome.

British immigration, I would discover that weekend, was not so gracious.

CHAPTER SIX

Chronicles from the Cell

London Heathrow Airport

Something didn't feel right when I touched down in London.

It wasn't hunger, although I hadn't eaten since I'd boarded the plane nearly nine hours before in Denver. It wasn't a nervous feeling either. It was a "caught off-guard" feeling. Like when you realize you left your phone at the restaurant. Or see the clock and notice your alarm didn't go off. I felt like I was forgetting something. But what?

As I walked off the plane, I ran a mental checklist of all the things I would need for the next hour. Luggage-retrieval tags? Check. Passport? Check. Turn-by-turn directions from the airport to my residence club, just in case the taxi driver didn't know? Check. Annotated notes of my new boss's job history and subject expertise? List of museums to visit when it rained? Check. Check.

I was still processing when I approached the immigration booth. Handing the officer my completed paperwork, I smiled and waited to answer the usual entry questions. Strangely they went on longer than usual.

"What's your purpose in England?"

"To intern at Z Communications."

"How much money do you have on your debit card? In your pockets?" "Do you have family in England?" "Do you have a letter from your new employer?"

"No. My company didn't say I needed that."

The questions continued until suddenly the guard leaned closer to me. Her voice changed from apathetic to stern. "I won't have that."

"W-what?"

"I am detaining you."

Detaining me?! My eyes widened as the officer seized a massive stamp and thrust it forcefully upon a dainty white paper. Nodding toward a hypersterilized bench several feet away, she added, "The guards will come for you in a moment."

It was a Saturday morning. I didn't know a single person on the entire island of the United Kingdom. My phone had an American SIM card and would cost me a fortune to call anyone, even if I had anyone to call. It was the middle of the night in Colorado. No one was even awake. Now what?

Twenty minutes and twenty thousand heartbeats later, two uniform-clad men arrived.

"Monika Lutz?" the first rumbled. "Please come with us."

"Wait. Where are we going? What's going on?"

They seized my bags and started to walk away. One grabbed my arm and nudged me forward. "Just follow him," he ordered.

The guards led me down winding white corridors into a room that I doubt is even on the airport map. *Why was I being treated like this?* I thought.

"Open your bags" was the command. With anxious willingness to prove my obedience, I mounted all three of my suitcases onto the gleaming silver table. *Zippppp, zip, zip,* and the seams busted open. Then I stepped back and watched a gentleman unload every item in every compartment of my luggage by hand, setting one after another on various tables until I saw every one of my possessions for my entire internship exposed before me.

Maybe they had a suspicion that I was illegally transporting something? But the United Kingdom and the United States have very similar laws. What could I have missed? I remembered my French friend who had been pulled aside in New York for the bottle of wine in his luggage that he had brought as a gift for his new host family. At age twenty he was legally allowed to have that wine when he left France, but in the United States, it was considered illegal possession. I ran lists in my head of all the common household objects that could have been considered illegal: fireworks, alkaline batteries, pocket knives…I didn't have any of those things.

"All right. All clear. You can put these back now," the guard announced.

I nodded quickly. Maybe if I obeyed these men they'd tell me what was actually going on. Hurriedly I squeezed every last piece back into my luggage. My reward was another male escort. So much for winning them over.

This time I was escorted through a new labyrinth of halls that presented another neutral-hued room so secure it took multiple passwords, swipes, and touch screens to get in. The officers took my bags into another room and instructed me to sit on a cold plastic bench.

"Get comfortable," he said, as he exited the room. "I'll send someone else to get you later." His heels clinked with torment as he walked away.

This must be the same clink that birds hear when the cage door locks, I thought. The echo delivered goose bumps to my skin. Lowering my head into my hands, I whispered in disbelief and bewilderment, "Now what?" The echo repeated my message. *Returned to sender.*

*   *   *

"Now press your ring finger."

"L-like this?" I never had been fingerprinted before—let alone under a single lightbulb in a two-way window-enclosed room. I couldn't stop thinking about who was watching me behind those windows.

"Your fingers are shaking. It's messing up the records. Do it again."

I nodded and restarted the process of rolling and sticking. Pressing and holding.

"Fine. Now come with me."

With stained digits, I entered another gloomy chamber. The first guard passed me to a second, Agent Willard Abila. I tried not to stare at his nametag, his steel-gray eyes, or his starched navy-blue uniform for fear that he would think me rude. Why did I feel so guilty for not knowing why this man thought I was guilty?

"Monika," his voice was so stern it made my own name sound incriminating, "I am going to ask you a series of questions. Answer the question and nothing more. Is that clear?"

My eyes met his to confirm my agreement but were quickly diverted back down in intimidation. I was an eighteen-year-old, American, girl. Alone in an interrogation room, a continent away from my home. How could I *not* agree to the officer's commands?

"First question: How do you feel?" The blue-brimmed officer bellowed at me.

I replied instantly, "Anxious. Rattled." *Stupid!* I thought. *Why would I say anxious? I didn't even know why I was here!*

The officer scribbled my response by hand after writing down his own question. Then, spinning the paper around, he jabbed at my two adjectives and barked, "Is that what you said?" I nodded. "Then sign here."

This became a redundant pattern. Ask. Write. Answer. Write. Speak. Sign here.

The room was so pitifully quiet that all I could hear was the pounding of my heart. Eventually the questions stopped, and I was sent back into the first dreadful chamber.

Forever passed.

The feeling of forgetfulness that I first experienced on the tarmac grew stronger, stronger, until Agent Abila reappeared. "We have decided that, despite your unawareness of needing to provide a work visa as an American to hold an internship here, we are denying your entry into the United Kingdom."

Shock overtook my body. My breathing became shallow and rapid. Unrelenting, he continued, "We are deporting you to Denver tomorrow morning at nine a.m."

My body rattled with heaving tears. *They're sending me home?* I thought. *What about my internship?*

Agent Abila didn't stop talking, "But because we believe you have been truthful to us, we will allow you to go to your hotel and return here two hours before your flight. Your previous flight fare, tonight's stay, your taxi fare to and from your hotel, and nutritional needs will be your responsibility."

I had paid out of my own pocket to be here. I wouldn't be able to afford another ticket from the United States to England. If I couldn't find a solution, I might never be able to return. The agents had all of my belongings, my American phone didn't work, and no one in the world knew where I was right now.

Agent Abila pretended he couldn't see me crying, couldn't hear me cough as I strained to choke out the tears from my throat and take each next breath. He persisted. "Sign here, agreeing to your consequence. Then you may return to your bench."

It was like signing my own eviction notice. But what option did I have? What else could I possibly do? I felt Agent Abila's steely eyes on me, intimidating my fingers into grasping the pen. The tip moved in slow motion as I watched it carve my name.

Now what?

*   *   *

Back on the bench, I heard the guards talking about me from their surveillance booth. "That poor thing. I have a daughter her age. I'd be infuriated if they were doing this to her."

I spun around. At that point I just wanted to see another human being who didn't want to deport me. I looked at them through the open door of their booth with my bloodshot eyes and noticed the female guard had a German last name. I spoke aloud without forethought, "Oh, are you German, too?"

She gave me a puzzled look. I continued rambling. "My dad's from Bavaria. My extended family still lives there. That's why I'm a dual citizen."

The guard stood up immediately and walked over to me with haste. "You're a German citizen? Then you don't need a work visa!"

I froze. She was exactly right. I'd taken my American passport because I'd just filed for my new German passport at the consulate in Los Angeles a few weeks before. They didn't return it to me before I'd left.

Ten minutes later the blue pressed uniform towered over me again. After explaining my passport situation, he remained unimpressed and somewhat mockingly declared, "If you can prove to me that you're a German citizen, I could revaluate the case." Then he left.

With those words, hope entered the detainment room.

The security guard dialed the number of the German embassy and gave me her phone.

I poured out my story to the man on the other end as soon as the line stopped ringing.

He calmly replied, "I am sorry to hear that, miss. Do you know that this is the security guard you are speaking to? The embassy is closed on weekends."

I groaned. "Is there an emergency number I can call? They're shipping me home tomorrow if I can't show proof of my German citizenship!"

"To *you* this is an emergency, miss. In actuality the United States is a very safe place."

My voice quivered.

"Miss, miss, please don't cry. Miss. OK..." He lowered his voice. "I do have one number I can give you."

I could hardly see the digits through my tears, but I hastily dialed. After I described my situation, the voice on the other line paused for a breath and sighed. "I wish I could help you, miss, but I can't access your documents until Monday. Even if I could get into the embassy, I don't have the permission to access any files. I'm sorry. There's nothing I can do until Monday."

Monday would be too late. My only choice was to go to my hotel.

The guard brought me my confiscated bags and unlocked door after door until I was out of the labyrinth. I turned behind me as the final portal slammed shut. In the tinted glass, I saw a haggard eighteen-year-old girl. Her face bitten by salty tears. Clothes, wrinkled and messy. Hands, clutching two heavy bags.

My first experience in London was far from a cup of tea.

*   *   *

"The last time I saw rain this bad was with my family in Frankfurt," I mumbled to my taxi driver. Frankfurt! I sat up in my seat. Another idea! Hastily I redialed the German official's phone.

"Is there any way you can convince the immigration officers to deport me to Frankfurt and not Denver? They've stopped listening to me."

"Acccctually." He paused, "that might work. Meet me at the embassy tonight. I will see if you have a chance."

I looked at the clock. It was 7:30 p.m. I had fourteen hours to save my internship.

After pulling a jammed ticket from the jaws of a machine at the Tube and riding the wrong bus, I arrived at Victoria Station. Now only a taxi stood between my internship in London and me. As the rain attacked me from every angle, every passing taxi was occupied.

So I ran. A thousand pitter-patters of my own feet later, something flickered in the night. Through the sheets of water, I saw a piece of fabric flapping amid the rain's brutal fingers. Yellow. Red. Black. The Republic of Germany!

I sloshed my way up the steps and remained in the waiting room. Ten. Fifteen. Twenty minutes slipped through my fingers as I sat shivering in the air-conditioned room. Whether it was my fear of being sent away from this place too or my wet clothing that was exposed to the chilly air that made me quake, I wasn't sure. What came next I could only pray for.

Finally he appeared. My bloodshot eyes, weak after my not eating for more than twenty hours and not getting any sleep for almost as long, widened to attention. A young gentleman, dressed casually, seated himself next to me.

"So now..." I could hear his subtle German accent already. "Tell me your story again, from the beginning."

I nodded and began to speak. Meanwhile, not a single emotion danced across his brow. He appeared unimpressed and unsympathetic. My nerves overtook me and I began to ramble, when he cut me off, looked me in the eyes and said, "Monika. Please relax. I will do everything I can to help you."

With those words, I hung my head, clenched my eyelids shut, and sputtered, "T-t-thank you." Evidently the Germany embassy employs angels.

He stated my options—go back to America and wait for my physical German passport to arrive in the mail or fly to Frankfurt, stay until the government offices opened, and acquire proper documentation to prove my citizenship.

I requested the latter. A plane trip to Germany was cheaper than a flight back to Denver. Since I was paying for my year on my own, I knew I wouldn't be able to buy another ticket from the USA to England. If I couldn't make this work, I'd lose my internship and my chance to return.

Hurriedly the gentleman called my German relatives for electronic documentation of their citizenship and confirmation of my relationship to them.

Gonggggg! The official handed me a temporary document as the clock struck midnight. "This will get you on a flight to Frankfurt instead of Denver," he said.

The small certificate transformed into a winning lotto ticket in my eyes. I nearly knelt to thank him.

For now I had to find my way home. With the help of two university students and a haggard old chap, I made it back to the door of my residence club.

It was locked.

As I stood in the rain, the sign shouted, RECEPTION CLOSES AT ELEVEN. WILL REOPEN AT EIGHT NEXT DAY. No phone number was listed. No back door indicated. Through the dark glass, I saw my luggage abandoned by the stairs, just where I had left it.

There, in the reflection of the window, I saw a new girl not present at the airport immigration office that day. Her hair was mopped from the rain, her clothing pulled by its fingers. But there was something else in her eyes this time—hope.

I banged on the door. Hollered. Pounded. Someone inside yelled, "Burglar!" Finally the handle gave. Behind its frame stood a sleep-covered man clutching a broom.

"Oh. Hello. It's too late to check-in," he mumbled through drowsy lips.

"No! Not checking in!" I replied with glee as I lunged toward my suitcases. "Just didn't get my key. That's all." I smiled.

"Oh, all right then. Come along."

I didn't want to unmake the bed for fear of having to check out the next morning. So I slept on the floor, completely dressed. My body was weak, my stomach empty, and my head still reeling from the adrenalin. In four hours I would rise again. My internship was on the line.

*   *   *

I raced along the walls of London Heathrow in my three-day-old damp and wrinkled outfit to find a single gray phone. I lifted the receiver. The agent was on his way.

My heart beat violently as Agent Abila's steel-gray eyes clutched me once again.

"Monika Lutz," he addressed me sternly, "do you have any new evidence?" He seized the temporary paper from the German embassy.

After touching every seam, running his fingers across every seal, and holding the document up to the light, he slowly mumbled to himself, "Well, look what the Germans did this time."

He got on his phone. "Sir, I have personally examined it. Affirmative. A dual citizen." He turned to me and spoke the words I had craved for twenty-four hours. "We have no reason to hold you here," he said. Then, with the turn of a heel, he vanished.

My heart was pounding. *Quick!* I thought. *Leave before he can change his mind!*

With my last bit of strength, I heaved my bags onto the Tube. Across the cobblestone. Up the winding stairwell. And into my room. There I collapsed to my knees and prayed.

I had nothing left. No more energy. No more strength. Not

a single trace of food in my system. I had only a simple realization that with insufficient planning and foresight, things can go wrong with the thrust of a stamp. But determination, dedication, and faith can make anything possible.

Now what? I was going to make it to my internship in London.

*   *   *

Before boarding the plane in Denver, I was worried I wouldn't be able to handle living alone abroad. Actually besides my detainment, the transition to England couldn't have been easier. London delivered the most academic, cultural, and artistic excitement possible with hardly any culture shock. In a single day's jaunt along the river, I saw *Henry IV* at Shakespeare's Globe, ate lunch at a local outdoor market, wandered through the Tate Modern museum, and ogled the Queen's jewels.

Training myself to check the opposite direction before crossing the street was simple. Even more, I spoke the language. Well, *most* of the language. I can't pretend I wasn't disappointed when I ordered sticky toffee pudding and a chocolate brownie arrived on my table. Lucky for me, that luscious combination of brownie, caramel, and oozing chocolate blew American pudding out of the kitchen, so I was only upset until I took my first bite.

At the office, I was grateful for an internal transfer from San Francisco that enabled me to work for Z Communications again. My clients were healthcare companies, which gave me an opportunity to learn about a new industry. Because London was a smaller office, I knew everyone by name and didn't encounter the challenges I had struggled with in San Francisco. I spent most of my days writing blogs, researching journalists, and writing press releases.

Indeed my London experience was defined more by the encounters outside of the office than inside it. I jogged along the Thames during sunset each evening, mesmerized by the shadows that the swans cast over the water. I lived in Richmond-upon-Thames, just outside of London, and within walking distance from work. I stayed in a residence club with a hefty breakfast included each morning for just six hundred pounds per month. By buying my other food from grocery stores (except for my sticky-toffee-pudding meal once a week, during half-priced happy hour, which I cut in two and ate for lunch the next day), I lived less expensively than I had in San Francisco.

I was absorbed in exploring the (only slightly) foreign country when an evening phone call blindsided me.

"Monika..." My mom's voice was somber. "Dad's flying to Germany right now. Your grandfather passed away last night."

I lowered myself onto a nearby bench in solemn surprise. I hadn't seen Opa in more than thirteen months because of my travels, but I still remembered every wrinkle on his war-wearied face. I could hardly speak his native language but when I pronounced a German sentence just right, those same wrinkles would weave themselves into a soft smile. Opa was the man who showed me the castles of Germany. Those rocky kingdoms whispered a childhood promise that princesses and fairytale endings really do exist. Now, the castles remained, but the man that gave them their magic would not be waiting by the drawbridge entrance for my yearly visit.

I swallowed hard, "Well, um, may he find rest and peace and, and lots of his favorite chocolates waiting for him in heaven," I finally answered, trying to be optimistic.

My mother sounded puzzled. "Opa gave up eating chocolate, Monika. Don't you remember?"

I frowned. Why didn't I remember more? A swan floated past me on the river. The phrase, "A rolling stone gathers no moss" rang in my ears. Life was continuing for my family and friends as I pursued my passions around the world. But how long could I be away before I forgot about their idiosyncrasies? While I was out discovering my dream life, whose life was I losing the opportunity to be a part of?

After I got off the phone with my mother, I started to list the friendships I wanted to maintain, regardless of where I was in the world. Frankly, with today's technological capabilities, there was no reason why I couldn't still share meaningful moments with the people I cared most about. I started to invest more time in e-mailing, Skyping, and calling friends.

Soon I began to feel closer to my friends than I had in high school. Probably since we didn't have time for pettiness or prioritizing other things, our conversations were more meaningful. When we were "together," we were really present. Granted, I don't know what they wore last week (that's what Instagram is for anyway, isn't it?) or what their birthday cake tasted like, but I was the first one on the phone to congratulate them on getting straight A's or coach them through rough times. My friends actually valued my opinion and advice more since I was detached from the situation and unbiased. Surprisingly, being away was becoming an advantage in my relationships.

The moon's slender light beams stroked another swan's silver wings as she swam beside my gravel path as I ran home that night. The sun had set for the last time on me in London. But my journey was far from over. New York City was calling me.

CHAPTER SEVEN

Special Victim Lutz

Flashback from New York City, 2009

I lifted my single suitcase up the cement stairwell to my New State University (NSU) dorm. Inside I saw two bedrooms, three closets, and one bathroom. In them five beds were buried somewhere beneath my new roommates' mounds of shopping bags, handbags, and luggage. Was I moving into a dorm or a war zone?

I pretended to be carving a path through the debris to my bed by examining various articles sprawled about. Cowgirl boots. Cigarettes. Crystal belly-button rings. My mind puzzled over with whom I would be confined to six hundred square feet for the summer when suddenly the door burst open.

Question answered—four distinctly fashionable girls stumbled in. They were all enrolled in a high school summer program at the Fashion Institute of Technology, according to their t-shirts.

It took me about three hours to figure out that "summer school" was only what they told their parents they were doing in the Big Apple. I raised my eyebrows as they gushed about what they *actually* did: drink, party, smoke, get tattoos and piercings, repeat. By the end of the night, it was clear that being seventeen and living in the same apartment was all that we had in common.

"Hey, girls, your stories are, um, interesting," I said, interrupting their storytelling. "But I've got my first day at work tomorrow, so I'm gonna hit the sack."

*   *   *

The next morning, in the center of Jefferson Park, I mechanically read *The Economist* while eating breakfast. Only a few words in, I noticed a shadow cast over my magazine.

Startled, I turn around to see a middle-aged, slightly balding Caucasian man behind me.

"Do you mind if I sit down? The other benches are full," he asked me.

"Sure." I returned to reading. Hardly half a minute passed before he interrupted again.

Outstretching his hand, he said in a friendly but unusually fast paced way, "Hi! I'm Daniel Ames! You're not from here, are you?"

Wanting to be polite, I responded with a laugh, "Nah, I'm from Colorado."

He handed me his business card. "I told you my name. You tell me yours."

"OK. It's Monika." I didn't understand why he had given me the card.

"So you're eating in Jefferson Park," he began quickly. "You must be staying at NSU. I used to go to NSU."

I wanted to stop talking. I had *The Economist* to read, after all. But that would be rude.

Daniel persisted. "It's summertime. You look young. Are you an intern?"

"Uh, yeah. I'm an in—"

He broke in, "You're beautiful, Monika!"

My stomach churned. That was it. I snatched my magazine, shoved my waffle back in the box, and shot up. "I'm late for work."

"No, Monika." He reached for my hand. "We were just getting to know each other. Please...stay longer!"

"No. Sorry." I stepped away from the bench.

"Well—how about a date? I'll call you!"

I was power walking through the park now. I waved at a group of students walking to class and pretended to know them. Leaning in closer to one of the girls, I whispered, "I need to get away from that man back there. Please, just let me walk with you."

She looked at me like I was crazy, but I kept up with her until I reached the edge of the park. There I broke off and charged toward my office.

*   *   *

My roommates were smoking cigarettes in front of our dorm when I came in from work a few nights later.

"Heeeeey! Monika!" they hollered between puffs. "How's your week going?"

"Um, OK. I met this guy in the park a few days ago and he...uh...he started talking to me. I don't know...It was a little weird. But he gave me his business card." I pulled it out of my bag. "I hope it's legitimate."

"O-M-G. That's cra-cra!" one of them said. "But whatevs. You'll be fine."

They went back to slurping long breaths from their cigarettes. I frowned at the card and went inside.

With work early tomorrow morning, I ran through my mental to-do list. *I'll call my boyfriend while running, then grab dinner. Eat while editing college essays. Then read and annotate the summer reading for my English class.*

I changed into my running gear, waved to the security guard on the way out, and dodged my roommates' smoke puffs as I took off down the concrete corridor.

*   *   *

Less than seven hours later, a forceful pounding hammered my door. "Open up. This is the police."

I flung myself out of bed and swung open the door. Two of my roommates stood in the hallway. Their makeup was smeared, and they were wearing nothing but flimsy underwear and bras.

"Are these girls your roommates?" he asked me sternly.

I squinted without my contacts. "Um. Yes. These girls live here." I avoided ownership terms. They shuffled past me as the officer left.

I closed the door, waiting for an explanation.

Valerie read my shocked expression. "I'll tell you after I'm done being...after I'm not so...ughhh." She groaned and collapsed into bed.

With the help of two Red Bulls, Valerie forced herself awake while I got dressed for work. Between sips, she told me the full story of her late night.

After I'd left for my run, Valerie and Bethany had gone barhopping with fake IDs. They met a few guys who bought them lots of drinks and eventually invited them to a house party. On the way there, one of the guys told Bethany that he was in love with her and wanted to get a tattoo to prove it. She watched while the tattoo artist inked her initials onto the body of the man she'd known for only a couple of hours. When it was finished, the man told her he had spent all his cash buying her drinks and didn't have enough to pay for the tattoo. Well coined, Bethany offered her parents' credit card, and the transaction went through. Then they took the train to his house—in New Jersey. A late night of partying ensued.

Around 4:00 a.m. the girls awoke to the sound of police banging on the door. "The owners of this house are wanted for credit card fraud," he told them.

"We...we don't know them. We just came here to party," they stammered. The girls' clothes (beyond their panties and bras), their wallets, and their purses had all been stolen. The house was abandoned.

The police officer drove them home and dropped them at our front door, where I stood at five thirty that morning.

I couldn't believe that's what girls my age did in NYC at night. *Looks like I'm going to have to spend my evenings alone from now on*, I told myself as I walked out the front door to work that morning.

*   *   *

Days later my cell phone rang at work. "Monika Lutz?" a stern voice asked. "This is NSU security. I need you to come back to your dorm immediately. Come in through the back door."

I sprinted out of the office. *Are they going to arrest my*

roommates or something? I asked myself. I started to recite my affidavit of not drinking or smoking while I replayed everything I knew about what my roommates had done earlier that week. Several nights had gone by. Who knew what trouble they had gotten themselves into since then?

When I arrived, the police officer ushered me into an interior security room. Window blinds darkened the space and a series of security televisions lined the wall. My feet pulsed from jogging the twelve blocks from my office in high-heeled shoes.

The officer began calmly, "Have you seen anyone hanging around you lately?"

My mind raced. Were my roommates letting convicts into our dorm? Was that what this was about? "Uh. No, no, sir. Not that I know of."

"Did you meet anyone in the park this week?"

A shiver ran down my spine. "Oh. Uh. Yes, sir. On Monday morning." Reaching for my bag, I pulled out a small piece of paper. "I have his business card. Here." The officer seized the card. A second officer stepped closer.

"Monika, if you saw this man again, would you recognize him?"

I nodded. The officer stepped to the side of the TVs. Each of them showed the same walkway in front of our dorm from various angles. A man paced across the screens—Daniel. My stomach dropped. What was he doing in front of my dorm? How did he know I lived here?

The police officer waited for my response. I nodded my head slowly, "Yes, sir. That...that's the man I met in the park."

The officer picked up a stack of envelopes and handed me one. "Will you read this please, Monika?"

Despite being confused by what he had just handed me, I nodded. Straightening out one handwritten letter, I began, "Monika, I came again for you today. I'm ready to go on our date..." I looked at the officer in disbelief.

"Keep reading, please."

I read every word in the thick stack of letters before me. As the minutes crept by, my perception of reality twisted. The author wrote about dreaming of me; he wrote about how beautiful I looked as I walked down Houston Street to work at 8:55 on Tuesday. He mentioned how much he also likes frozen yogurt from FroYog where I went after work on Wednesday...

I dropped the papers into my lap. I was sick to my stomach. I just couldn't keep reading.

The officer began again. "Monika, this man has been coming to your dorm multiple times a day for the past week. At first he just brought letters or would ask to leave you notes. Today he demanded that we let him wait in your room. When I refused, he told me that he's dating you. This man appears to be in his mid-forties. Our records show that you're seventeen. Monika, are you having intimate relations with this man?"

My body went numb. My conversation with Daniel had lasted only a few minutes. How could he say we were *dating*?

"No, sir. Absolutely not." My voice started to quiver. My mind raced. I retold the details of my encounter at the park. The time of day. Our exchange of words. Until that moment, I hadn't told anyone except my roommates.

"Monika, we have reason to believe this man is stalking you. We're not sure of his intentions, but he seems very persistent. We recommend you move out and remain under special protection until we decide you're no longer in danger."

I nodded my head quickly, searching the officer's face for a look of sympathy. I received none.

Instead undercover agents waited to relocate me. I ran upstairs to pack. No one else was home. I didn't have time to wait for my roommates. Besides, no one could know that I was leaving. Everything had to appear as though nothing had changed.

Within an hour, my side of the dorm room was bare. I was escorted out by T-shirt-wearing police officers and transported to my new apartment. My emotions shifted between shock, fear, and isolation. Who could help me now? My parents would be more afraid than me.

As soon as the police left me in my new apartment, I called my brother, Norbert. I was petrified to turn on the lights in my room for fear that someone would know I was home. I had to squint to find his number in the dark.

The first ring made only a whispering sound in my ear. I had turned the volume down low so that no one could overhear from the hallway. A second whisper arrived. My family never talked about relationships. But here I was, calling to tell my brother that his little sister was alone in New York City and being followed by an old man who'd fallen in love with her. I had no idea how to break the news to him. Finally, I heard the click of the receiver being lifted off its cradle.

"Hey, Monika." Norbert's voice was casual.

I jumped in. "Hi. I need you to be really calm right now and listen to everything I'm about to say."

His voice lowered with suspicion. "Uh, OK. I'm listening."

I began to speaking. As I did so, I felt a touch of security in the double-locked, sealed, and empty room. I recapped the meeting in the park and added, "The police think I'm being stalked, and I've been put under their protection. I—"

"Wha...?" He interrupted me. "No, OK. Go on."

"I'm standing in my new apartment now. It's on the seventeenth floor on the other side of town. I closed the windows and had the officers check under my bed and in my closet, but..." My previously matter-of-fact voice began to quiver. "But how do I know if I'm..." I swallowed hard, "...safe?"

I leaned my shoulders against the faded walls. Their hard surface pressing against my back filled me with the sensation of being protected. It meant that no one was behind me, that a single side of my body was secure. "I know I should feel better that he can't watch me through my window anymore, but I can't help thinking, *All the way up here, who would hear me scream?*"

"Who else knows about this?" Norbert asked, apparently more confused than afraid.

I told him all the details then continued, "I'm so scared. I'm so paranoid. I didn't know he was around before—how could I know it now?"

I was young. Vulnerable. Alone. My brother had disapproved of my interning in New York for these reasons before I even had signed the contract. Now I was proving him right. My impressive luxury real estate marketing internship didn't make me bulletproof. It proved to him that I couldn't live alone without getting into trouble. That I was still just his little baby sister.

"Monika, I understand that you don't want Mom and Dad to worry but you have to tell them before NSU does."

I gazed into my dark room and visualized the soft purple paint of my parents' bedroom. I imagined the phone ringing from their bedside. My mother would turn over in bed to pick up the receiver and hear the voice on the other line tell her that her daughter was being stalked nearly two thousand miles away in New York City. I could see the look in her eyes, the silence as she listened to the voice. I felt nauseous.

I had to make that call. Mom picked up. When I finished retelling the events, the line was silent.

"Fly home," Mom said.

"No," Dad interrupted. "You can't run away from this. You can't get him arrested unless he physically harms you. Ask the police to help you bait him into the park, then get him locked away and stop worrying."

I ended the call more confused than when it had begun. Now what?

I had earned my seat at a luxury real estate marketing firm after several interviews and working tirelessly in my high school activities—from founding the business club, to training our team for state business competitions, to interning for a Boulder startup the summer before. I had gone through so many hurdles. Was I supposed to abandon it all? I was organizing a photo shoot for a historic hotel account at work. I was learning so much and never would have the same opportunities back home. I couldn't quit now.

Meanwhile the prospect of seeing Daniel again made me sick. I was so confused. I circled the perimeter of my room like a goldfish in her new tank. The lights were still off, but my eyes had adjusted.

Then I realized, at the end of the day, this was *my* life. I couldn't always depend on other's opinions to guide me—even if I loved and respected them. I needed to listen to my heart.

I called my parents back. Speaking at normal volume, I began, "I won't let one man change my life," I told them. "I can't give up on my commitments or this incredible opportunity because I'm afraid. I'm going to complete my internship." I softened the blow by promising to cooperate with the Special Victims Unit (SVU).

After all maybe I was just overreacting. The next day I met with the head of the SVU to find out.

Her deep-brown eyes looked me cold in the face. "Monika, I'll be straightforward. A summer student last year didn't listen to us when she got stalked. Now she's not around to tell anyone about it."

My face went white. "You're the expert," I said. "Tell me what to do."

Her glance softened. "From now on our agents will drive you to work and meals. You'll tell me your daily plans and be home by sunset every night. Keep an erratic schedule. Don't let anything about you become predictable."

I nodded slowly and stood up to leave. That was all my nerves could handle.

That night I greeted my new security guard, Vincent, when I got home. After my other guard had reported the stalker, I wanted to be friends with the new one. On Vincent's desk was a colored paper with a picture.

"Oooh, new guard update?" I asked nosily.

"Hmm, I haven't even looked at it yet actually." He unburied the sheet. I saw my own image gazing back at me with the subtitle, "Alert: new special victim student. Please make accommodations."

I froze. I never thought a situation like this would happen to me. How could one five-minute conversation change so much in my life? Every security agent on campus knew me after that. Soon SVU held the top spot on my phone's most frequently called list, above my boyfriend and parents.

By the time I boarded my flight home to Denver, Daniel had yet to reappear to me. Since he did not physically harm me, the police could not arrest him. In my calculations, that was ok. I preferred to endure the psychological trauma associated with the aftermath of our first meeting than to endure a physical assault for the purpose of having him thrown in jail.

Being away from home proved how easy it was to stumble into a situation that I never had encountered growing up in a small, safe town. That first internship in New York taught me more than just solid marketing skills and how to make big decisions for myself. It taught me that safety should never be an afterthought.

*   *   *

One year later, as I sent my acceptance e-mail for a new fashion communications internship in NYC, I hesitated. What if I ran into Daniel again? I was fortunate to leave the city last time with nothing more than a psychological spook. Was I tempting fate by returning?

Monika, I thought, *there are millions of people in New York City and probably dozens of them who have bad intentions for teenage girls.* Was I going to let the possibility of running into one of them stop me from pursuing what might be my dream career? No.

Instead, I was going to take the job and every precaution possible: travel in groups, get an apartment far away from where I had lived before, carry pepper spray, never walk home alone late at night, never talk to strangers, never wear high heels to or from the office, never talk on my phone at night when walking home, and learn to kickbox.

Collapsing my umbrella and tucking the last of my clothes into a suitcase above the murmur of British voices rising from the apartment below, I mentally prepared for moving back to the Big Apple. But street smarts and personal-defense tactics couldn't protect me from bad internships, as I was about to find out.

CHAPTER EIGHT

Big Apple Internship Gone Rotten:
Eighteen and Unemployed

New York City

A wrong address was only the first misleading bit of information from my new boss. The "team" was actually the president, founder, and owner (all one person) and another intern who was twenty-four years old. The "office hours" revolved around the intensity of their party circuit from the night before. The "administrative staff" was a barista who made inappropriate jokes about me while my boss and coworker giggled from barstools just feet away. I got free peppermint steamers as long as I put up with his taunting.

When another customer's gargantuan mocha latte sprawled on my notebook one morning, I couldn't contain my frustration. *How did I end up here?* I fumed.

Through quite a bit of work actually. I spent my weekends in San Francisco combing through FreeFashionInternships.com and other online internship boards, looking for fashion public relations internships. I thought social media would be the wave of the future, so I looked for opportunities to blog and learn the digital communications trade.

The process was time demanding and daunting. I researched each firm before sending them a personalized, thoughtful cover letter that read like a story but articulated why I was a good fit for their specific firm. Usually one application a day was all I could find time for. It took approximately ten applications, four responses, and six interviews for every one position I was offered.

I was rejected left and right. "You're eighteen. No." Or "I don't care if you're *moving* to New York. Don't contact me until you're here." The strongest words came from the editor of a famous magazine who took the time to write me a verbose paragraph beginning with, "Get some actual experience before you try to get into this industry." And ending with, "don't ever waste another editor's time with your ten-page résumé."

I collected all their responses and incorporated them into my future appeals. For this specific internship, I proposed a project to interview the firm's fashion-designer clients and create a podcast of discussions that I could then blog about and post on their websites. Abby, who eventually became my boss, loved the idea. She offered me the position via phone and I agreed to start in November.

Now weeks had gone by, and all the projects I proposed were met with, "Maybe next week you can start on that. For now I want you to do this for me..." Week after week my boss told to delay my projects to make way for small, personal tasks she needed done.

Today I had reached my emotional climax. Alone on my fire escape, I reread the recent e-mail from my boss.

Hi, Monika. Hope you're feeling better. I just wanted you to know that going home because you have a headache is unacceptable. I'm disappointed you didn't stick it out. Just so you know, if want to make it in the fashion industry, you're going to have to be stronger than that. —Abby

"Unacceptable"? I shook my head in disbelief. Five hours earlier, around 3:00 p.m., my migraine had reached a painful height. The sneering of the barista and screeching cappuccino machines in the coffee shop where we worked had pushed it over the edge.

I had walked up to my boss and said, "Abby, this migraine I mentioned earlier just won't go away. It's really hard for me to write these blogs for you while my head is pounding." I motioned to the brigade of squawking coffee appliances. "Can I go home, take some Tylenol, and deliver this blog to you tonight?"

Abby and the other intern nodded their heads apologetically. "Yes," Abby replied sweetly. "Feel better!"

Now home, I puffed a steaming cloud of hot breath into

the frigid winter air as I reread the e-mail she had sent just minutes after she had excused me. I delivered the blog, as promised, and my head cleared up. Apparently the situation at work had not. "Since when is asking permission, getting approval, and submitting the deliverable in advance unacceptable?" I thought out loud. "And why didn't she tell me she disapproved when she dismissed me?"

This stunk. I had cut my London internship short to be here. Now the toxic environment and piles of false truths had become too much. I wasn't allowed to start on the project I was hired to do. My office was a noisy, crowded coffee shop. And a verbally abusive barista gave me more guidance on my tasks (even if they were all negative) than my boss did. My Big Apple internship was rotten.

Now what? I exhaled and peered into the night sky. The only light came from little scars of starlight flickering above a sphere of light pollution.

I needed to make a decision—continue working for my current firm and spend the next six weeks hating my job or quit and hope I could get another one. Six weeks is hardly an obstacle to overcome in a lifetime. But in a gap year, it constituted eight percent of what might have been the only year in my life that I could do anything, anywhere—as long as I could make it happen.

I stood up on my fire escape. The Empire State Building glistened in the distance with such confidence and fortitude that I remembered why I had come to New York in the first place— for an internship that would reveal to me whether NYC, fashion, and communications was where I wanted to spend my life.

In the hazy veil of the moonlight on that frozen, black metal fire escape, I made a decision—I was going to quit.

I wasted no time. After ripping open the contacts list in my phone, I e-mailed the real estate marketing firm where I had interned last summer. I intentionally had kept in touch with them, so I knew that social media was a hot topic for them. I asked whether I could pitch them on a social media campaign for their current accounts. Having written for several publications now, I stood a chance of convincing them to take me on as a consultant. It was worth a try.

But first I was going to endure my first quitting.

*   *   *

By 9:00 a.m. on Monday, I was at the coffee shop, despite my not having received a reply from Abby regarding the starting time for the day. I endured the barista's morning jabs until ten thirty before texting and e-mailing Abby again. No reply. The other intern didn't show up. *They must have gone out together the night before*, I thought. This wasn't the first time.

Meanwhile, back at my apartment, my parents had come to visit me for a few days and were waiting to see me. Being away from them for three months made me miss them. Sitting overdressed in a coffee shop while being hit on by a thirty-eight-year-old bald man instead of showing my parents the Big Apple only frustrated me more.

Disgruntled, I e-mailed my boss again.

Hi, Abby. Still waiting for you here at the coffee shop. I feel that my time is being disrespected because you haven't notified me of our start time while Nicole [the other intern] obviously has been. I came in today to speak with you about a particular topic. Please call me at your earliest convenience. Thank you.

I forcefully tapped "Send," zipped my laptop case closed and ducked out of the suffocating coffee shop. I stopped on the corner to take a look at the door I never wanted to pass through again.

*   *   *

Two hours later, the call came.

"Did you *leave*?" Abby's Italian-American voice was aggressive.

"Yes, Abby." I tried to sound sweet, but my frustration

was audible. "I was waiting alone for over an hour and a half with no indication from you about when work would start. Having made multiple attempts, I left the coffee shop."

"Yeah. Saw your e-mail. *You* feel 'disrespected'? We need to talk about this."

"Absolutely." I glanced at the scratch paper on which I had sketched out my reasons for quitting. An arrow ran from "mention erratic schedule" to "factors have been misrepresented." My finger followed along as I began slowly, "Abby, I came to New York to work personally with fashion designers, as we agreed upon, in a learning-conducive and positive environment. So far every time I ask about the project you hired me for, you say, 'Next week.' I understand that we never signed a paper contract, but I feel that these factors have been misrepresented to me, so I'm discontinuing my internship." I held my head high to keep my voice confident, but my nervous eyes gave me away. Luckily she was only on the phone.

"Oh, yeah?" Abby's speech was noticeably faster now. "Well, I feel disrespected that you aren't more grateful to me for taking a chance on you. I think you should know that you're not cut out for this industry in the first place. There's no need for you to come back."

I shook my head in disbelief at her defensiveness. "Thank you, Abby." Click.

Three weeks into working in New York City and I was unemployed.

*   *   *

To my disappointment, the Monday-evening phone call I was expecting from my old firm didn't come. Just in case it never came, I opened my address book and e-mailed firms I previously had worked for, online internship websites, friends in the city—any and all of the people who could give me information about open positions for which I could interview. The reality of quitting my internship was settling in, but knowing I wouldn't have to return to endure another day of harassment and misrepresentation made it seem worthwhile.

"One more e-mail, and I'll take you to see the tree in Rockefeller Plaza, OK?" I negotiated with my parents. They nodded and continued to eat omelets off the only two plates I owned.

At first, I was worried my parents would think I was a quitter for leaving the internship. To my surprise, their response was just the opposite. "Never stay in a bad situation to please others, Monika," they told me the day before I quit. "Besides, this year is about discovering what *you* want, not about pleasing *us*. As long as you find the next internship and pay your rental checks on time, you don't have to ask us for permission to leave a company."

Having my parents stay with me was a special treat, since I'd only ever lived in dorms or residence clubs before then. It was an honor to show them my new life: the apartment I was paying for, the dinners I could cook from scratch, the new city I was calling home. I could tell by way they treated me that the initial tension with my gap year was fading. In its place was a newfound respect; their daughter was independent and happy, the outcome they'd both wanted all along.

On Tuesday my parents departed, leaving my apartment empty. So too was my inbox and voice mail. I reloaded my web browser. I tested the phone system. Nothing.

I was getting nervous. I needed to have a backup if I couldn't find an internship. With my test scores, maybe I could tutor students in economics or French while I scrambled to find full-time work. A Google-fest for contact names and best practices ensued. I filled out the online classifieds and other task-specific profiles. Then I hit the phones, calling high schools in the area and pitching my services.

I got two replies that stated, "You're on our list. Thank you." Hm. Not exactly putting food on the table.

Wednesday wandered to midday, when I was told my consulting offer at the real estate marketing firm was, "On the table and would be reviewed again in the upcoming weeks." That would be too late! I only had a little more than two months left in

New York. My airplane ticket home was already paid for so I couldn't return to Boulder early. In the meantime what would I do in New York?

I followed up on e-mails and calls then reached out to the companies I had turned down in order to intern at the fashion PR firm. I left no professional contact unturned. Not even *Glitter Magazine*. I reread the editor's e-mail from July. "Monika. Get some actual experience before you try to get into this industry. And don't ever waste another editor's time with your ten-page résumé." While it stung upon initial response, I smiled now. This editor had told me everything he wanted to see.

I hit "Reply" to the e-mail and began, "Dear Mr. Mullen, I contacted you several months ago to express interest in an internship with your magazine. At that time you recommended I gain additional experience and fine-tune my résumé before circling back with you..." I went on to outline the ways in which I had fulfilled all of his recommendations, then concluded, "I am still interested in an internship with *Glitter Magazine* and would be pleased to meet you in person for an interview. Thank you for your consideration." *Send.*

Meanwhile, no new offers had arrived. It was too dark to go jogging, so I partook in the only other relaxation method I knew—I called my brother.

"No college education. No school affiliation. No lead-up time. And an apartment to pay for that's slipping bills out of my pocket at each sunset. Norbert, what would you do if you were in my situation?"

"Well, have you tried—"

"Everything!" I cut him off anxiously. "I feel like I've exhausted every option and can only wait! I'm so nervous! How could I think I could get another job this fast? Who do I think I am?"

He paused to think, then responded exactly as I needed him to. "You know, Monika, fear creates the gaps that separate you from God. Now, I can't help you do this. But God can get you a job by Friday. I'm leading a Bible study tonight. Can I have our Cru study group pray for you?" My heart lifted as he went on.

"Keep doing everything you can, Monika, and have faith."

After the phone call ended, I let my cell phone slip out of my hands as I sank to my knees on the cold floor. As if squeezing my eyes shut would bring me closer to Him, I prayed, "Jesus, I can't do this on my own. I don't know where I'm going to end up." Saying it out loud set the reality in stone. "But please promise me you'll put me where you want me. I trust you." I exhaled. The weight lifted from my shoulders and I drifted off to sleep.

*　　　*　　　*

On Thursday morning I pushed my cereal around my bowl for several minutes; I was engaged in a staring contest with my cell phone on the other side of the table. There were no new e-mails all morning. Hence my phone was winning.

Ding! I shoved the bowl across the table and lunged for my phone. It was an e-mail from a couture fashion designer I had tried to intern with earlier in the year. "Can you come in for an interview on Friday morning?" I eagerly confirmed the appointment. *All you need is one, Monika!* I told myself.

Ding! "Monika, I am impressed by your persistence. How does Friday look for an interview?" Signed: Mullen@GLITTERmag.com. I raised my eyebrows in disbelief. Persistence? Maybe that's all I needed to pull this off!

By Friday morning I had multiple interviews lined up. The first had potential but grew sour when they learned I'd only be in New York City for another two months. Since there was nothing I could do about it for the moment, I tucked their contact information away for future summer internships and put reminders in my calendar to check in with them.

The second interview with an haute couture fashion designer was a complete flop. Despite having done thorough research on my interviewer, the collection, and recent relevant news about the brand, I never could have predicted the cold company culture. My interviewer didn't greet me at the door but rather yelled across the room at me when I entered, "Turn right,

Blondie. And take a seat." Her stiletto heels where so high and sharp that they could double as daggers.

She began, "Are you're here to do the work listed on the job posting?"

Slightly startled, I replied, "Yes, ma'am. You said you were looking for an organized, dedicated marketing intern to work on the London Fashion We—"

She cut me off. "Uh-huh. OK. Those projects we mentioned, yeah—those are *potential* projects. Seriously, though, we're looking for someone to iron the clothes and organize our racks before they go to the shoots."

Not exactly a career-enriching experience, in my opinion. After eyeing the bullet points on my pre-interview prep sheet, I presented a unique, personalized blogging opportunity I could instead do with the designer to build his brand awareness. I also discussed a complementary social media extension we could add later.

The leather-pants-wielding interviewer rolled her eyes. "Look. Social Media isn't posh, like us. Again, we need an ironer."

While I was willing to start from the bottom and work my way up, compromising my standards regarding a positive work environment and opportunities to learn wasn't acceptable. "OK," I said. "I understand. Thank you for your time."

The sun was nearly behind the skyline now, and I had nothing to show for it.

At my final interview for an internship with Current, an influential communications firm, I made a friendly joke with the security guard.

Through a thick accent she replied, "I see a lot of interns walk out dem doors, gurl. I hope you one of 'em that come back."

I gulped. "Me too. Me. Too."

Round one. I had Googled my first interviewer in advance and began with my usual opening to break the ice. "Adam, I noticed you have experience working in the Office of the Attorney General in Austin, Texas. What pulled you away from that and towards Current?" From there I showed my dedication by adding why I wanted to work for *this* communications company rather than any of its competitors.

After hearing his story, I transitioned to my golden question. "What are you looking for in your new team member?" I wrote down all the adjectives, experience, and skills he mentioned and addressed how I met each one. Then I discussed a value-adding project proposal I could start working on during my first day. That showed my creativity and eagerness to help the team.

Two. Three. Four more colleagues took a swing at interviewing me before I waved good-bye to the security guard on the way out.

As I stumbled with fatigue into my dark apartment that night, I was in mid e-mail to the vice president of the company. "Hello, Nina!" I wrote. "The thank-you card is in the mail, but I just wanted to send a digital note of appreciation..." I needed to show that I really cared and wanted to be at the top of their inbox on Monday morning.

I hit "Send," dropped my backpack, and sunk onto my bed. Without even opening my eyes, I tore into a bag of gummy worms. On autopilot I dropped one high-sucrose candy after another into my mouth. After I'd finished off nearly the entire package, my phone dinged.

"Great to meet you today, Monika. You impressed my team. I'm calling headquarters now to confirm your position. Can you start Monday?"

I sprung up in bed. The time stamp read 9:48 p.m. on Friday. "A job by Friday!" I heard my brother's voice ring in my ears. *He* did it! We did it!

I called Norbert while jumping on my bed. "It happened! It's Friday night and I'm employed!" As if an entire bag of gummy worms hadn't spiked my energy level enough, now I was full of adrenalin. I was beaming. I couldn't believe this blessing!

Life, yet again, had worked itself out perfectly.

Monday morning was the first day of my most professionally rewarding internship to date. Initially I thought that two months wouldn't be enough time for me to have a valuable experience. In actuality the relatively short time period gave me a sense of immediacy to achieve something and the pressure to learn all that I could. My direct supervisor, Adam, had the ideal combination of traits for a boss; he was near my age but professionally skilled far beyond his years, patient, and trusting.

The solid foundation I had acquired at Z Communications enabled me to jump right in without having to be trained. With the holidays coming up, our biggest accounts needed a lot of extra attention, and my team graciously passed the opportunities my way.

Nearly two months later, I wandered around the Christmas tree in front of my apartment building at sunrise. Community members had tied pieces of paper to its branches in response to the question "What does 'New York' mean to you?"

After grasping the dog-chewed pencil to answer, I scratched, "That unbelievable feats are possible with persistence, faith, and dedication."

I tucked the fragile scrap into the branches and rolled my suitcase down the sidewalk. I had a flight to Denver to catch.

As soon as I returned home, my trust in faith and fate would be tested again; it was time to reapply to college.

CHAPTER NINE

Boulder and College Apps: We Meet Again

Boulder, Colorado

Before flying home to Colorado, I visited Alexander, one of my closest friends from high school, at his new home: Princeton University.

Sitting in a dining hall plucked from the set of a Harry Potter movie, Alexander handed me a mug wrapped in tissue paper. After uncovering the navy-blue porcelain cup inside, I read the inscription—"It is my destiny."

The words struck a nerve. Alexander, wearing his blaring orange Princeton shirt, sat down next to me at the commanding maple table. "We're celebrating the anniversary of my dorm, so they gave me this mug. I know how much going to Princeton meant to you, so I wanted you to have it."

I looked again at the mug in my hands and tried to take in the situation. I remembered the way my heart had broken on April 2nd when Alexander ran up to me in class, his arms spread wide, and shouted, "Mon! We're gonna be classmates *again*!" He didn't know I'd been rejected.

Now, staying in the dorms, eating in the cafeterias, and running around the castle-like campus felt like I was experiencing the life I could have had if Princeton had accepted me a year earlier.

Strangely, the longing for Princeton I had harbored for four years was nowhere to be found. The grade deflation, the excruciating competition, and the sheer stress of class made my current life sound far more fun. *How had I been so lucky?* I asked myself. *Why did I have the good fortune to go explore the world and myself instead of enduring the daily grind of campus life?*

"It is my destiny." I stared at those four words. That's just it! Not getting in was the best thing that ever happened to me. It *was* my destiny! If I hadn't been rejected from college, I never would have experienced India or Nepal or living in San Francisco and London. If I hadn't been rejected, I'd still be thinking my self-worth could be judged on a GPA scale. I couldn't wait to share these new realizations with my community back home.

*   *   *

Coming back to the Boulder area was a bittersweet awakening. Without my realizing it, the world I'd left behind had changed a great deal. I was concerned about challenging myself, discovering my real passion, and exploring the world. By contrast, my old friends worried about grades, parties, and getting into the best fraternities.

"Gosh, Monika, it must be so hard for you to come back here and see all of us moving on in our education while you're left behind," Ashley, a friend from high school, told me over a morning tea on Pearl Street. "Don't you regret that you'll be graduating after all of us already have jobs and are beginning our real lives?"

I repeated her words—"left behind," "real lives." I didn't feel left behind in the slightest! The way I saw it, I wasn't waiting four years to start living my "real life." I was already.

"Wait, Ashley, we were just talking about your rush to get through classes so you can 'finally' start living your dreams." I paused, "I don't want to sound harsh, but if you were willing to put your 'dream life' on hold to go to college, what makes you think you won't let your next job delay it even further?"

Ashley's hazel eyes gave me a look of confusion. I went on, "Look, after you graduate, you're probably going to marry Matt [her high school sweetheart]. He's got his own dream career in mind. At that point you'll say that 'It's not the time to leave on a gap year because we can't make any big changes while we're just starting out.' What I've seen again and again during my year is that the spiral continues until you've forgotten what it could ever mean to have a year to yourself, to explore who you are and what's best for you."

Ashley set down her drink and replied sharply, "Monika, you've been gone for a while," she said. "Let me remind you that the sequence of events is: high school, college, job, life. You have to go to school before you can get out, and I just don't understand why you'd want to delay that process any longer."

"Ashley, what's one year in the span of your entire life?" I pushed my bubble tea to the other side of the wire table and continued, "No, seriously. How well spent would that one year be if it saves you four years and thousands of dollars on a degree in a field that you discover you hate as soon as you've broken in? That's already happened to me!" I pivoted in my seat, then continued, "Now how will that one year pay off in five years when you realize you have to stick with the poorly fit job you *thought* you wanted just to pay off the student loans you took out to be academically qualified to get there in the first place?"

Ashley looked down and swiped at her iPhone screen. My words had hit home. Before we'd started talking about my gap year, Ashley was telling me about her frustration with her current major and the pressure of living up to her parents' plans for her life.

"Ashley, you're so eager to ensure you weren't left behind by the crowd that you forgot to consider how taking a year to do internships would have taught you in *six* weeks that you hate your current major! And what about your parents? They probably would've been proud of your getting the internships and excelling in a field of study. Then you wouldn't have to keep feeling torn between trying to please them and your heart." I exhaled, realizing I might have struck too many nerves at once.

A frown crossed Ashley's face. "This is how things have always been done, Monika."

I nodded, realizing I wasn't making any progress. *Just because something always has been done a certain way doesn't mean it's the best way to do it*, I reasoned. Deep down I felt that my gap year was a way to beat the standard post–high school track of aimlessly wandering through majors and career fairs. However, it was clear that not all my friends agreed with my approach.

Variations of my conversation with Ashley occurred again and again as my time back at home continued on. After each one, I reflected on the complaints my friends shared. Then, under the shadow of the Flatirons, I sat typing my essays, Common Application, and personal statements for college. Although I had gone through this process before, it felt radically different now. My activities, interests, and desires had changed in so many ways.

For the "activities" section, instead of discussing how I'd spent my last break coaching a lacrosse camp, I detailed my internship experiences abroad. This would show the admissions staff that I had taken real actions to pursue what I wanted to study. The work I did on my gap year demonstrated maturity, initiative, and promise for the value I would bring to the classroom. Now that I was confident in what I wanted to study, I wouldn't fall into the "wild card major" pile, where all the other "undecided" applications end up.

I was eager to get back to school. Learning seemed like a welcome respite from the demands of work life that didn't come with multiple-choice answers. I remembered countless hours during my internships of swarming around a boardroom table analyzing which of any hundred actions should be taken to solve a problem. In those moments I longed for my textbooks, my professors, and my lecture halls, because I knew they had a correct answer in mind.

This time I focused on finding a school that would fill in the gaps of my education that I had discovered while interning. I wanted a school that fit me, not a school that I would do everything I could to fit into. I applied to only a few schools, based on available majors, extracurricular offerings, proximity to a metropolis, and recommendations from respected employers and colleagues.

After a week of essay writing and editing, I hit "Submit," closed my laptop, and went on living my life. From my eyes now, college was just another steppingstone. Besides, I had bigger things to worry about at the moment. Like what to wear during my four-month marketing internship with a fashion designer in Shanghai.

CHAPTER TEN

Making the Cut: Fashion Design in China

Shanghai, People's Republic of China

Standing beneath a bulky black box, I gazed up at its one-word digitized message—SHANGHAI. My mind confirmed what my heart hadn't yet. I was actually moving to China.

I suddenly came to my senses. I spoke less than two-dozen Chinese words. I knew nothing of what life in Shanghai would be like. I didn't even know the names of the roommates I'd be living with for the next four months! What was I thinking?

I refocused my attention outside, where the sun was just peeking above the horizon. In my line of sight arched an accordion of a walkway without an attached plane. Its open mouth revealed a harsh drop to the tarmac. *Is that what would happen to me today?* I thought to myself. *Would my American life come to an abrupt halt as I ventured fifteen time zones away? Was I leaving everything I loved only to gain "life experience?"*

The universe answered my questions for me. "Seating area two. Last call for seating area two."

*   *   *

Thirteen hours later I stood in the wide avenue that encircled People's Square. The area was crammed with Chinese citizens. They darted across the street. Smoked cigarettes like it was their job. And looked on as their children huffed with all their might to send opalescent bubbles into the smog-ridden midday sky.

I weaved through them on my way to my apartment. I was here to work for a famous fashion designer on her marketing projects in preparation for Shanghai Fashion Week. At night I would study Mandarin in an attempt to comprehend the solely character-ridden menu at a local restaurant whose ingredients I was only partially certain I wanted to know.

Thankfully, I wasn't alone. Soon after my arrival, my four male flat mates became brother-like figures. In total we could practically play a game of poker with our plethora of passports: Danish-Italian, Iraqi-Mauritian, Chinese-Indian, Chinese-American. And me, an American-German.

"Nah, nah, nah. That's not how it's done..." James Blond, my affectionate term for the Danish-Italian, corrected Pavir, the Chinese-Indian, on his technic for using chopsticks. I had walked in on what I would soon consider a standard dinner debate.

With such diverse upbringings among all of us, everything was up for debate. Suddenly I was an unofficial spokesperson of the United States. How I treated other people, my values, how I felt about certain politics, and the types of questions I asked could all change my roommates' perception of America. I felt the need to be educated for the sake of being able to answer their questions. Fortunately, no matter how heated the discussion, at the end we knew we were the closest thing to family any of us had in China.

To add another dimension, being the only woman among four men made me an adopted member of the lineage but with limited hereditary rights, so to speak. The guys acted as my protectors but made it clear that I would be playing by their rules. This included mandatory late-night movies (which were all action-packed thrillers, of course) and soccer games (called "football," because I was the only American who called it "soccer"). I cheered for their team (Arsenal). They trained me in chess and poker—as long I always gracefully lost.

"Enough explosions and Daniel Craig for tonight, boys." I yawned and got up off the couch. "I've got work tomorrow morning." I waited for them to wave goodnight. Instead they grunted in unison and shooed me away so I would stop blocking their view of the television. Apparently just being invited to movie night was enough to convey that they cared about me.

Eight hours later I struggled to squeeze in between seventy other people in the subway car bound for my office. The experience made me pity sardines. Pressed from every angle, I grew bored of watching the person in front of me play Angry Birds on his phone. Instead I practiced my Chinese words via a deck of homemade flash cards. This started what became a daily game—team flash cards.

It began with me quietly reading a word aloud to myself. Usually the person shoved up against me in the crowded train, as curious humans do, would peer over my shoulder. When I got a word wrong, he would correct me, "*Bu shi, bu shi.*"

At my making such a beginner's mistake, the other passengers would overhear, chuckle, and watch for the next card. Almost immediately after it surfaced, a stranger would yell the answer. "*Gui!*"

Of course the person was always correct. So I'd smile and repeat what he or she had said. "*Gui.*"

Select members of the crowd would then cover their mouths and laugh politely at my poor pronunciation. I enjoyed the game because it helped my accent but couldn't deny that I felt like a street performer working for laughs.

Our game continued until my last stop, when I would slip the cards back into my pocket, and wave good-bye, "*Zai jian! Zai jian!*" Those in the cabin waved back.

The next person to wave to me was the security guard at my new office.

Promptly he ushered me into a modern boardroom where Michelle, my internship program coordinator, waited for me. Frosted glass framed the walls, and modern chairs encircled the table where full-colored images of The Designer's latest line appeared. She was famous for her attention to detail and mythical designs. Her previous season's show had transformed several white materials into three-dimensional gowns resembling swans. The intricate craftsmanship made chiffon layers appear to be real feathers lunging toward the onlooker.

"You're here for a marketing internship, right Monika?" Michelle asked before turning back to translate to The Designer.

I nodded.

"Great. The Designer will walk you over to meet the team, and then you can jump in!"

Despite submitting an English résumé and receiving English confirmation that I'd been accepted, there was only one other English speaker in the entire thirty-person firm—the other intern. After just nine minutes of meeting my Mandarin-speaking colleagues in the marketing department, it was blatantly obvious that I wouldn't be able to create an ad campaign in Chinese.

I'd only been at work a few hours and my internship was turning out to be more than words could express—mostly because I didn't know any (Chinese).

Soon, through the international language of charades, my new boss told me to pick up my stapler, note pad, and pens and follow her to the other side of the building. We passed racks strewn with couture clothes, picture boards, and material bolts and arrived at a naked wooden desk illuminated by streaks of musty sunlight. This was the design desk for the team of five artists that created all the drawings for The Designer to select for her shows. My boss handed me an example of a dress design and fresh stack of blank paper. On the top sheet, she scribbled down the number "10".

I nodded, smiled, and politely sat down at the chair she designated for me. Then, as soon as she turned her back, I scooted over to the other intern.

"What does '10' mean?" I whispered to him.

He smiled kindly and laughed. "That's the number of designs you need to draw every day and submit to The Designer. At the end of each week, The Designer will come over and critique your pieces. Draw them by hand, and the ones she likes will be modeled digitally." He pointed to the example drawing The Designer had given me and turned back to his work.

Was I a designer now? I puzzled to myself, *but I thought I was here to do marketing!* With my eyes, I followed the maze of clothing racks back to the marketing division. Without being able to speak Chinese, I was of little use to them. *Maybe the international language of pictures would be the best way to add value to the firm*, I concluded.

This seemed like fun! As a little kid, I liked sketching wedding gowns on my notebooks. Thanks to my Fashion Institute of Technology roommates in New York City the summer before, I knew how to draw mannequins and clothing. If my new boss simply wanted to see how I would interpret her designs and add an American flare, I was qualified for the job. After all how hard could it be to create ten designs a day?

Very demanding, I discovered. I wanted to bring in local style but found it confusing. The women here loved cute things. Fuzzy pink pens. Sweaters with puppies embroidered on them. Those little pom-pom fuzz balls that go along the hems of dresses. They absolutely *loved* them. Hello Kitty was basically the Chinese equivalent of a pin-up girl. She adorned everything from my colleagues' backpacks to their pens, their iPhones, and note pads. But for some reason, every time I attempted a cutesy design, it seemed awkward to me. Nonetheless, I added them to my designs in an attempt to fit in.

After the first week, as promised, The Designer approached me to review my designs. Her face was youthful and delicate like fine porcelain. She moved calmly, fluidly, with an understated grace. Like an afternoon autumn breeze, she flowed through the studio; each person felt her presence, but none were disturbed.

After examining each of my designs, she smiled. Then she replaced them in a neat stack on my desk and took a large rubber eraser out of her pocket. After setting it on top of my pile of designs, she politely pushed them back toward me and walked away. I got the hint.

I worked extra hard that week. By the end, The Designer made her regularly scheduled trip to my desk. Her long fingernails communicated her upper-class status of not having to do manual labor. She leafed though my designs and separated them into two piles, a surprising twist to her usual eraser offering. I waited in anticipation. Holding two of them, she murmured a, "*Hao.*" Then she walked away.

I scooted my chair over to the other intern. "What just happened?" I whispered, trying to be discreet.

He smiled back and leaned in to whisper, "She liked them!"

My eyes lit up with excitement.

"Now she'll put them into the pile for the team to draw out a pattern. Then a third team will select the material. The next time you see it, it'll be on the racks!"

The next day I learned firsthand that the process wasn't so "seamless." In fact getting a design selected required attention to detail unlike any I'd experienced. For example, simply drawing a button onto one of my designs wasn't a sufficient enough description for the production team. I added, "Red button here," thinking that would fix the problem.

The swarm of follow-up questions proved me wrong. Did I mean a quarter-sized button or a dime-sized button? Was it round, square, or hexagonal? Was it fire red, light red, or slightly red? Would the button be plastic, metal, or wood? Would there be two, three, or four holes?

At one point, The Designer, the translating intern, and I spent an entire workday shuffling from one clothing district to the next searching for the simple button that would adorn the pants I'd designed. When I got home that night, I decided I'd use zippers for the rest of my life. I couldn't look at another button.

Since I was the same dress size as their target audience, whenever any new design was finally produced, the team asked me to try it on. I was filled with excitement as The Designer, two seamstresses, and several other artists circled around me. *What are they looking at?* I wondered.

To them the cloth hanging off my body wasn't intended to simply cover my skin. It was supposed to convey a message. Was I endorsing the current trends or contrasting them? Did I add a new twist to the "it look" or was I creating one of my own? Was I staying true to the promise that my label delivered? Did I appeal to a new market or was I watering down the brand?

The Designer whispered a command. In response the seamstresses lunged toward me. They lifted my arms at different heights. Brushed my hair wherever they wanted it. Pinched different parts of my clothes, tacking them with pins or sticking them with bits of tape. More commands ensued, and before long I was draped in measuring tape like a present in the midst of a seven-year-old's gift-wrapping practice.

When I finally trudged back to my eraser-covered desk, I felt guilty, not glamorous. Deep down I couldn't overcome the truth that I hadn't come to China to be a fashion designer. The glitz and mystique of the job were overshadowed by fatigue from my never-ending task of sketching (which was mostly erasing, if I'm honest) and the citywide scavenger hunts for the perfect fabric.

Monika, I reprimanded myself, *you're being spoiled. How many girls in the world would give anything to see the designs they doodle in the margins of their homework on the catwalk at Shanghai Fashion Week?* Something had to be wrong with me.

More likely the reality that I wasn't fashion-designer material was setting in. I was nowhere as talented as the drawing wizards who sat beside me at the design desk. My fascination with promotions and price points and competitive analysis instead of pea coats and pinching and couture made it obvious that I wasn't learning what I needed for my future.

Now what? Would I stay at work for the next two months to learn more and more about a job that was wrong for me? Or would I quit to get on a path that was closer to my career goals? Working at an internship that wasn't an optimal fit wasn't wrong, but staying there when I knew I wasn't learning the skills I'd come to China for would be.

In a few days, I confirmed my decision. So long, Shanghai Fashion Week.

Fortunately, ending my internship didn't jeopardize my ability to stay in the country. I had signed a four-month internship and housing agreement with Next Step Connections, an internship placement company I'd found online. They had offered me an academic scholarship, coordinated my housing, and helped me secure a visa. I called Michelle, my coordinator, and explained the situation. In times like these, the support of an organized company was vital.

The next day two firms called me for interviews.

"Thanks for coming along, Michelle!" I exhaled with relief as she walked me to my second interview. Although English was the native tongue of the office this time, Michelle still accompanied in case anything needed to be negotiated in Mandarin. Over the months of her being my coordinator, she had become more of a respected friend than an assigned staffer. She often took me to local food hotspots, taught me Chinese card games, and even helped me book travel tickets. Her accompaniment now calmed my anxiety that I would end up in another firm where no one understood me—literally.

A week of interviews later, I signed up with a worldwide healthcare marketing firm.

*   *   *

Life in my new healthcare marketing office was starkly different than that of the design firm. Here everyone spoke English, and I liked the academic challenge that linking the medical and consumer fields required.

"We need to understand how this new product compares to our competitor before we can start the brainstorming process," my boss announced at our meeting the first morning. The room was silent.

Curious, I returned to my desk to research the products from a biological standpoint. The first few white papers were surprisingly easy to understand. *Hey*, I thought, *I remember some of this stuff from my International Baccalaureate higher-level biochemistry class last year.* I continued to scan the plethora of research documents. *Wait, the way the body absorbs these drugs is different! That carries serious implications for efficacy!* A year ago I thought biochemistry was just homework. Now I had a way of adding value that my colleagues hadn't realized yet. Being submersed in the pharmaceutical industry was actually bringing my schoolwork to life!

Jacob, my boss, called me into his office to share my insights. Between the two of us, we represented the entire expatriate population in the office. This created a bond between us.

He pointed to my research notes. "This is good work, Monika. Now tell me something else. Do you eat frozen yogurt?" he said casually but with authority.

"FroYo? Of course! I love it! It has active cultures that improve digestion and a lower fat content than ice cream." I paused. "Um, why do you ask?"

"Because a new frozen yogurt pitch is coming up. The food hasn't really caught on in China yet, so we need someone with personal experience with it."

"But we're a healthcare marketing firm," I said. "How does an ice cream competitor hold up next to arthritis medicine in our portfolio?"

"The company wants us to position it as a health food. You said it yourself, 'active cultures and less fat.' The board of directors is flying in from America this month for us to pitch a campaign to them." He tossed a packet of company information, facedown, onto my side of the table. "We'll need you to run due diligence, presentation creation, and briefing notes for the team. Be ready to explain this to us next week so we're all on board. You get us up to speed, and we'll put our resident MD's on it for the finishing touches. Call me if you have questions." His phone rang. "That's my one p.m. call. Excuse me." He nodded toward the door to hint at my departure.

I nodded too, took the info packet off the table, and ducked out of the frosted-glass office. I'd worked on several marketing pitches at previous companies and knew the series of events, but did he really just give me an entire account to prepare!?

I sat down at my desk and turned the information packet over. The bright logo of a famous American frozen yogurt brand stared back at me. My eyes bulged.

The responsibility was a little overwhelming. "OK, Mon," I said to myself at my desk. "Just start from the beginning. What do people think about frozen yogurt? Is it a dessert? A healthy snack? Where can they find it? How much are they willing to pay for it? What type of person would eat it? Has anyone gotten sick or healed from frozen yogurt lately?"

I shoved everything else on my desk to the side and furiously began to research. In doing so I found an appreciation for one of the values of my American society—internet freedom. When I was looking for some simple background information, I couldn't solicit Wikipedia. When I needed to watch a video about how frozen yogurt was made, YouTube wasn't patiently waiting for me. When news updates in fewer than 140 characters was all I needed to understand public sentiment about a particular event, Twitter was nowhere to be found.

I had to think outside the Internet. In twenty minutes I was in downtown at the six-story shopping mall. The Chinese love their shopping malls. With a note pad and some Chinese ice cream terms, I sprang up conversations with the servers. I interviewed customers and vendors at various price brackets to find out preferences, special ingredients, trends, government regulations, et cetera. I needed firsthand insight to back up online findings. This was heaven for me—practicing Chinese, getting ice cream samples, and learning, all at the same time.

During the following weeks, I continued on-site, in-person, and online research and prepared the entire presentation for the board of directors' visit. I was so submersed in my work that the fateful day came sooner than expected.

"Monika, please meet our board." A sharply dressed executive took me down the line of four directors as we bowed to one another.

Thank goodness we weren't shaking hands, because mine were trembling from nervousness. I couldn't believe I was about to pitch the decision makers of such a famous company.

Now, as I stood alongside my Chinese boss, our dance of traditional Chinese business etiquette felt awkward. Here I was, an American greeting other Americans. But because we were in China, we bowed to one another. We accepted business cards with two hands and gazed at them for several seconds before setting them on the table in front of us. We even served lukewarm water because the Chinese think it's more special than cold.

Under dimmed lights and the glare of a PowerPoint presentation, we gracefully progressed through the pitch exactly as planned. Since I was the most familiar with their product from the United States and most knowledgeable about the content of the presentation, the directors questioned me personally.

The member with distinguished-looking black hair and a jutting jawbone started. "Monika, can you tell me how you think the public would perceive an American brand coming into Shanghai?"

Does he know he's asking an eighteen-year-old for advice? I thought. Actually what did age matter? Here I was, surrounded by marketing veterans, but I understood something no number of years on the job had taught them about—American culture and frozen yogurt. I knew the product. I knew the market. I knew everything that was needed to dazzle this client. This wasn't about age; this was about playing to my advantages.

I summed up the confidence to respond, "Mr. Montie, the recent infant powdered-milk calamity has made citizens extremely paranoid of Chinese products. Foreign brands, especially in the dairy industry, now carry a seal of confidence and security that Chinese citizens crave. Judging by the preliminary data we've collected, your frozen yogurt would be in high demand."

The questions continued for nearly twenty minutes. When the visitors walked to the elevator afterward, my boss and I waved good-bye until the doors shut. The moment the steel jaws clamped closed, he threw his hand up for a massive high five.

"Way to go, Monika!" he cheered me.

I beamed. I wanted so badly to make my team proud. I could hardly believe such an opportunity would come across my desk. Only a few short weeks ago, this whole project was just a briefing packet. Now, all those pep talks in the bathroom mirror to get over my jitters finally had paid off. The combination of stepping up to the challenges I received, dedicating my energy, and giving my best seemed to be a winning combination.

I went back to my desk that afternoon heavy with the

fatigue that accompanies a job well done.

At the desk next to me, my colleague was turning the page on her paper wall calendar. Looking back at me, she smiled and said, "Can you believe tomorrow will be April already?"

"April first?" I repeated quietly. A chill ran down my spine. "One year ago tomorrow, everything changed for me."

CHAPTER ELEVEN

"Rejection Day" No Longer

Hanoi, Vietnam

After 2010 I had decided to call April 1st "Celebration of Rejection Day." Just being able to say the word "rejection" proved that I was emotionally healed from the experience and realized that having all my dreams shatter at once was the best thing that could have happened to me.

Thankfully, Celebration of Rejection Day 2011 didn't bring rejection. When the Skype camera turned on that morning, I saw my parents holding several large manila envelopes. I looked at them in disbelief.

"Wait... I... Does this mean?"

"Yes, Monika!" my dad replied with a full, fatherly smile. "You've been accepted!" He pointed at one. "And the dean from this one sent me an e-mail—you've been awarded the only Dean's Scholarship! This one is offering you forty thousand dollars. These two said you've been accepted to their honors programs." He paused. "And look what else, Mon." A giant "H" filled my screen.

The acceptance letters answered my questions regarding what the admissions committees thought about my year off. Through travel and internships, I had shown clear initiative and determination. Most likely, my international and professional experience filled a niche in their student body.

I looked back at the letters, partially in disbelief that this moment would ever come. I had only ever experienced rejection from the colleges I'd wanted to attend.

My mom continued, "By September, Monika, you'll be going to college! You got the best of both worlds—a gap year to discover yourself *and* your school choice!"

When our call ended, I quietly closed my laptop and sat softly on my bed. Memories of April 1, 2010 sprinted through my mind. I saw the e-mails again. I saw the orange ribbon in my hair. I remembered everything about that moment. But the sounds, the feelings, and the emotions were gone. All the disappointment, rage, and dishonor I'd felt so vividly that day was missing—just like at the Vipassana meditation retreat several months before.

As the awareness of the acceptance letters returned, the reason became clear. A year ago this would have been my ultimate moment of happiness. A year ago, I'd thought this would be the crowning moment in which my future trajectory would be determined. But now it felt deeply ironic; after I'd given up college idolatry and traveled the world to find an identity of my own that was separate from grades, test scores, and status, the colleges actually wanted *me* now.

I left on a gap year to avenge those feelings of disappointment, inferiority, and failure. I left to prove to the Ivies that I *was* good enough for them. But now the person I had proved it to was *myself.*

I finally got in! Now what? I was ready to go back to school because I realized how much more I needed to learn. I knew I wanted to study Mandarin Chinese and had nearly a full semester of the language under my belt from living in Shanghai and working with a Mandarin tutor twice a week.

The opportunity to learn from the world and discover what I loved to do before going to study it—"reverse education," as I called it—felt like the right path for me. I needed a school that would enable me to continue interning abroad while earning credit for my degree. Harvard, through The Extension School, would offer me just that. My classes for the next year would be occurring on campus and filmed live so I could watch them in real time wherever I was in the world. I'd have dedicated teaching fellows to coordinate me and ensure that I was learning along with the rest of the class.

The university fit my spiritual and academic requirements; it had a strong Christian campus ministry (Cru), a fantastic government program, and professors who were leading experts on China. It also offered the opportunity to earn a double minor in Mandarin and general management. Socially I needed to be surrounded by other students who were dedicated academics but valued social interactions and life outside of the classroom. Harvard checked that box. Geographically all my travels had assured me that I wanted to be on the East Coast and very close to but not directly in a big city—everything that Cambridge is to Boston.

One of the things my gap year revealed is that obsession with a particular school isn't a prerequisite for admission. In fact while I was an Ivy League–obsessed high-school overachiever, I was rejected from college. It was after I left on a gap year to follow my own passions and discover myself that I discovered there are alternate routes to reaching my Ivy League educational goals.

I spent no time wallowing in indecision. I knew exactly what I wanted my next four years to look like. I'd continue to intern during the week, travel on weekends, and take classes from Harvard Extension School as a distance student. Then I'd move to campus. That way I felt as though I'd be getting the best of all worlds: travel, academic education, life education, and professional education. This would enable me to break out of the harshly defined lines of what "higher education has to be" or "what study abroad has to include." I wanted to see whether it was possible to do all of these at once.

For the moment I needed to renew my visa in order to stay in China, which required leaving the country and then reentering. "Where's my backpack?" I asked the empty room. I planned to backpack through the rice paddy fields of Vietnam for four days, guided by a local and sleeping in his friends' homes. After this past year, I figured Harvard could wait another six days before hearing from me again.

*   *   *

Soon after I stepped off the train platform in Vietnam, I neared the edge of a cliff. Below me, rice paddy fields clung to the edge of the mountain, plunging more than a thousand feet downward. I was in the northern mountains, suspended in a cloud.

I inched toward a light. There was only one. It was a single lightbulb, dangling from a feeble wire. I would have moved faster, but it was nearly 10:00 p.m. and the fog was so thick that my limbs were invisible. A gust of light wind splashed droplets in my eyes as I pulled them open further and further in hopes that I could collect more information regarding my surroundings.

My attempts were useless. The only figure I could make out was the lightbulb. In the thick fog, its rays were spliced into a diamond formation that shot in each direction of the compass rose. One beam struck me directly.

As I inched closer, the silhouette of a bony tree appeared, and the train I had just evacuated collapsed behind me like a stage prop. A familiar metaphor played out literally—with each step toward this foggy light, I had to abandon what I knew from behind me. Staying in safety was the most comfortable position. I was afraid. I was unprepared. But I had a burning desire. I had to know what it was like over there!

One blind step after another, I reached the light and my senses were restored.

These moments of misunderstanding, these attempts to comprehend—wasn't this the essence of my gap year? Why was it that after twelve months of constant globetrotting, it had taken a common meteorological occurrence, stretched to the extreme, to remind me what my journey was all about? This moment helped me make sense of who I was and where I stood in the world. At this instant the world was anything I wanted it to be.

*　　*　　*

One tear-off calendar on the bamboo-wooded wall at a local's home was my only reminder that I still lived in the same real world that I'd left behind in Boulder. We'd spent days traversing emerald hills and rickety wooden bridges to reach the homes of local hosts who poured us fresh ginger tea so pungent our tear ducts nearly burst. Vietnam was a trip to explore a new culture and remind me that happiness and security were not manufactured in ivory towers or dispersed via manila envelope. Rather, they are found in things not earned and yet enjoyed— family, nature, and life.

I'd now walked through the clouds of my gap year, not sure where to put my next step, but infinitely curious as to how far I could really go. How much fear could I overcome? What was on the other side? As I was about to find out, these hills were a mere step of the much longer excursion ahead. Back in Shanghai next week, the road was about to get very bumpy.

CHAPTER TWELVE

Keep Your Enemies Closer

Shanghai, People's Republic of China

The majority of those bumps were in my personal life.

Before leaving on my gap year, I told myself that distance wouldn't impact my relationship with my high school sweetheart, Gordon. I was right. It wasn't the distance. It was the growth. The gap year was especially hard for me while I was in a relationship, because as I opened my mind to new countries, lifestyles, and paths, my dreams and directions changed. So too did the definition of the person I wanted alongside me in that journey.

The biggest struggle was that, in every new location, Gordon had to encounter all of the new characters, environments, and struggles in my life from behind a wall of glass. It was as if he could observe everything, but never actually be there with me. Our relationship had become a series of updates and daily reruns delivered via Skype. It was hard for him to comprehend what my new life in each place was like. And when he finally started to see how it all came together, I would move again.

After we'd spent a full year apart, the cracks between Gordon and me burst. Now there were no more strings from high school attached to me. My college dreams, my dog, my awards, and now my sweetheart—the most important parts of my pre-gap year life were all gone.

With so many changes, I grew especially close to my roommates in China. If only I'd remembered the forewarning of a fortune cookie I'd eaten in Boulder before departing. "Keep your friends close," it read. "Keep your enemies closer."

By late April, Shanghai's sudden snow flurries and constant dreariness had inspired me to book a weekend trip to the island of Sanya. To my surprise my Chinese-American and Iraqi-Mauritian roommates, Allan and TC, decided to come along.

A few months before, that would have been OK with me. Now Allan's presence made me nervous. When Allan had moved in, he was quiet and observant. Now, pressure to turn his internship into a job offer was pushing him over the edge. He drank more and more, cursed, and started fights in nightclubs and on the basketball court. As soon as the glass hit his lips, he lost control of his five-eleven, two-hundred-pound frame.

The first day on the beach in Sanya, TC and I sat down at one of the plastic tables that lined the shore. Russians ran the beach, hollered, and drank among themselves. Without invitation, Allan toppled into the chair next to me and ordered hard drinks, one after another.

TC and I continued our conversation. Just because Allan had crashed our lunch didn't mean we had to listen to his profane commentary. Allan, however, couldn't stand being excluded, so he sought attention any way he could. "Monika," he said, "do you know why all these people are looking at you?"

"Um, because I'm blonde," I replied bluntly. "Chinese people have been asking me for pictures for months. This isn't new." I went back to talking with TC.

"No!" he exclaimed. "It's because you look like a wh*re"

I immediately turned to TC. "Did he just call me that? That's enough. I *cannot* handle you anymore, Allan," I bolted out of my seat and onto the beach.

From the sand, I watched Allan talk to TC while he reached for my drink. Within minutes, TC shot out of his seat and walked toward me. He kept his face looking straight ahead and forcefully nudged my arm. "Let's just walk away from here, OK?" Believing him, I did.

After a few moments, TC leaned in. "Do you trust me?" His deep-brown eyes looked forceful.

"Of...of course." Our roommate group was so close that the question startled me. "I've lived, eaten, and hung out with you every day for three months now."

"Good. Then trust me when I say, 'Watch your back when we return to Shanghai.' And know that it wasn't me."

I stopped immediately and looked him squarely in the eyes. "TC, *what* are you talking about?" What had Allan told him at the table while I was away?

"I don't know what Allan will actually do. But he's capable of a lot." He slowed his walk and lowered his voice. "And he's talking about taking advantage of you."

"TC!" I yanked my arm back and raised my voice. I had reached my wit's end with Allan's shenanigans. "This is getting ridiculous! You and the other guys *have* to do something about this. If I confront him with only your hearsay, he'll know you told me, and he'll turn his rage against *both* of us."

"Monika, look." He placed his hand on my shoulder and lowered his voice. "Allan's completely unpredictable and doesn't realize how aggressive he is when he's drunk. If one of us confronts him, there's no telling how violent he could get. It's best not to do anything until he actually crosses the line."

I had moved to China knowing I'd be living with complete strangers. I'd opened up to them over time, and they were now some of my closest friends. But things had gone so well with the first three that I didn't expect that opening up to the fourth meant that I had exposed myself too much. Was I actually living with someone who had bad intentions for me?

I looked at TC in shock. I couldn't believe he wasn't going to stand up to Allan. I would have to take all of this on by myself.

*   *   *

Fortunately our flight back to Shanghai left the next morning. Back in the apartment, Allan's presence evoked a quiet fear in me. He was too difficult of a person to be friends with, but the flipside of not being on good terms with him was potentially dangerous.

I had no reason to be afraid until something actually happened, so I spent the next few days in paranoia. When I got back from work on Wednesday, the waiting game ended.

Thirsty from a long day, I reached into my cupboard for a drink. We each had our own cupboards in the kitchen to reduce confusion. I pulled out a bottle of my carbonated orange juice from its storage location and poured it into a clear plastic cup.

With one sip, a burning sting tore down my throat. *Yuck. Is this rotten?* I wondered. *It couldn't be. It's carbonated orange juice. I just bought this after we got back from Sanya.* I tried one more sip and sniffed the glass afterward.

It wasn't rotten. It was spiked.

"Anyone home?" I hollered into the empty apartment. I shoved the door to the kitchen shut, smelled the drink again, and quietly opened Allan's cabinet. Inside, there was nothing but half-filled hard liquor bottles and some ramen noodles—the foundation of his diet. Typical Allan. I grabbed the first bottle off the shelf, slipped off the lid, and inhaled. The odor was identical to that of my orange juice.

Spiking my drinks? Is this what TC was talking about? I felt sick to my stomach. Would my roommate, a member of my family away from home, really try to take advantage of me? Afraid that someone would enter the apartment and catch me opening Allan's cabinet, I replaced the alcohol, poured my orange juice down the sink, and rushed into my room.

I locked the door and sunk to the floor, with my back pressed against it. What had I done to Allan except leave the table after he insulted me?

Now what? Who could I trust? If I told my roommates, would they protect me? Or would that only start an actual fight? Was this the worst Allan had in store for me or only the beginning? As my roommate, he had access to all my food and practically every other possession of mine. The potential for damage was enormous.

I texted TC, "We need to talk when you get home." I couldn't handle the situation alone.

I went out into the evening smog that surrounded my balcony, where no one who entered the apartment could hear me, and called Michelle. "I've had a situation in the apartment," I said. "Can I meet you at your office in twenty minutes to discuss it?"

My blunt opening to the conversation startled her. "Uh... Monika? Yes. Of course. Is everything—"

I hung up the phone. I needed to get out of the apartment before anyone came in so it wouldn't be obvious that I had wised up to Allan's tricks.

Since Michelle and I spent so much time together, it wouldn't seem out of place for me to meet with her at the last minute. Her round, hazelnut eyes met me at the door with curiosity and ushered me into the conference room. She had barely closed the door when I began to recap the situation.

The founder of Next Step Connections, Jerome, knew me as the scholarship winner and observed my hurried entrance from across the room. He sheepishly poked his head into the conference room. "Is everything OK, Monika?"

I motioned him to sit down and continued to debrief them. "I don't want Allan to get into trouble, because I don't want him retaliating. I just don't know how much further he'll go. I know I'm completely exposed in the apartment and—"

Jerome interrupted with a voice of honest concern. "Monika, I'm so sorry. We've never had a situation like this before." He exchanged glances with Michelle, who nodded, and continued, "I'm afraid that if we expel him now, without proof that it was him who spiked the drink or what his intentions really are, he will only retaliate. What if he goes after the other interns thinking they tattled on him?"

I remained silent.

He paused, then offered, "We do have a new apartment that we're opening up. It's slightly nicer than the one you're in now and on the other side of the city. Why don't I call Allan and let him know that since he'll be here the longest, we want to upgrade him to a better apartment?"

I relaxed a little. "Ok, good. Then we can all play the 'roommates who have to stay behind while he gets upgraded' game, and none of the other interns will suspect anything." I nodded, pulling nervously at my pearl necklace.

"Exactly," Jerome said. "I'll call him after work today and have him moved out by the weekend." A look of concern flashed over his face. "Until then please, be careful."

When I got back to the apartment, TC was the only one home. His dark-curly hair and deep-brown eyes watched me enter the living room. He didn't need to speak for me to know that he was inquiring about my text message.

I brushed past him smoothly and tilted my head toward the kitchen. As he followed me, I poured a fresh glass of my orange juice half full and offered it to him. "Care for a drink?" I raised my eyebrows but drained my voice of any emotion.

TC eyed me, confused. His wide eyes focused on the drink, then back up at my face, before he cautiously accepted it. "All right," he spoke in his thick Oxford accent. Raising it slowly to his tan lips, he took a quick swig and winced. After slamming it onto the counter, he gulped hard and looked at me in amazement. "Bloody hell! Are you trying to choke me? That must be eighty proof!"

"Shhhh!" I quieted him, afraid another roommate might hear him on his way into the complex. Then sarcastically I whispered, "Why don't you ask our roommate? He seems to think himself a dignified bartender these days."

"He wasn't joking, was he?" TC looked down at the glass, then up at me. "Are you OK?"

"I called Michelle. They're going to move him. But what else does he have in mind?"

"That's the worst part. There's no telling." TC heaved a long sigh in the direction of the glass. "All right. We're eating out until he's moved out. And I'm staying here with you when they all go out. The last thing I want is Allan coming home first when you're alone." He touched my shoulder. "Come on now. Clean up this glass and bottle so everything looks normal."

Just as I tossed the liquid down the sink, Allan burst through the door.

"Phew! Such a hard day at work. This investment banking stuff is whipppping me. I could use a drink." He pushed past me, grabbed an entire bottle of vodka by the bottle's throat, and clamored into his room without offering even a greeting.

Is this really how he's going to play it off? I asked myself. TC casually shuffled a deck of cards at the table, as usual. I sat down next to him.

From his room, Allan hollered, "Oh, hey, Monika. I got some new Chinese-language podcasts today. I know you like those."

Since when does he know what I like? I thought. I didn't look up from the table. "Good to know. Thanks, Allan."

Allan walked into the living room and stood just a few feet from where I was. "If you want, later tonight I could help you with them while everyone's out for dinner or somethi—" His iPhone interrupted the invitation.

"Oh, it's Jerome. Hold up." He slammed his door and took the call.

I scooted my chair closer to TC and whispered, "I can't figure him out! Does he think I'm *so* dumb that I'd actually be alone with him after what he said in Sanya and what he did to my drin—"

Allan flung his door open. "Booyah! Jerome's upgrading me to another apartment. Who wants to go out and hit the town to celebrate?"

Considering my track record of not drinking with the boys, I knew he wasn't talking to me. I took the opportunity to distract myself with my phone and restrain my desire to look at him in absolute bewilderment. How could he act so normal with such tricks up his sleeve? Regardless, I was going to stick by my other roommates.

The sun sprinted another lap across the smog-ridden sky before finally passing her torch back to the stars. By then, Allan was gone.

The bitter taste of betrayed trust, however, was still in my mouth. *Could I have seen this coming?* I asked myself during a routine afternoon run between rusty bicycles, street food vending carts, and congested alleyways. Perhaps I should have insisted on an all-female apartment. That wouldn't have the same benefits of male brother figures to protect me when we walked back from dinner late at night, though. Besides, the other three male roommates were wonderful. Allan's incident must be what happens when I play with statistics—the more roommates I get, the more chances I'll have that one of them will be bad. Perhaps I should have notified my coordinator sooner and asked to move at the first sign. I just kept thinking Allan would change, that the stress would pass and he'd never act on his mean words or foul jokes. Maybe I over-reacted. Did I call in for help too soon? Maybe nothing would have happened anyway, I reasoned.

In the distance, I could see the antenna of my coordinator's office building. I nodded my head with confidence. It was right to act as soon as the actions started. No one ever would give me a medal for "refusing to be intimidated in the face of danger." Meanwhile, if I had waited and been harmed, I would have to bear the scars. Clearly, trusting my instincts, communicating with my other roommates, and building a good relationship with my coordinator were the best actions to take in resolving the situation and guarding against future mishaps.

*   *   *

A few weeks later, I wrote thank-you notes to the colleagues who had impacted me the most and finished the final day of my internship. My other roommates, Pavir and James Blond, did the same. Their rooms, usually cluttered with clothes and souvenirs, had been barren for days by the time I left for the airport.

Since TC was the only roommate remaining, he accompanied me in the cab as it whisked me away from my Chinese home. We tried to joke about typical things and keep the subject away from the reality that I was leaving. I traced the skyline over and over with my eyes. To say that Shanghai was rapidly developing is to insult the city's neck-breaking pace. The landscape, neighborhoods, and infrastructure were in such constant flux that the leading guidebooks had to release a new version for the city every year. I wanted to remember every groove before time resculpted it. Shanghai would no doubt change significantly before I returned.

But so would I. Leaving Shanghai felt like leaving my family. Being outsiders in a sea of Chinese people had made each of us roommates bond closer to one another. Since we all had come from different places, there was very little chance we'd ever see each other again. This was most likely the last time TC and I would be together in person. I admired the gleaming yellow stripes on his well-pressed polo shirt and the perfect helices of his black hair as he waved goodbye. This image would be the TC that would live on in my mind until we met again. With each additional step he took away from me, a tear was pulled further down my porcelain cheek. I was tugging at the final punctuation marks of my closing chapter in China. I knew that as soon as I stepped foot on that airplane, I would never have another moment to rewrite it.

Slowly, I made my way to the security check. I tucked my plane ticket and passport into my special travel folder. Beneath them sat screen shots of my college acceptance letters.

The echoes of voices from Rejection Day the year before ricocheted off the inner walls of my head while I waited for my airplane. *You're just running away, Monika. What will colleges and employers think of you? How could you disadvantage yourself by graduating a whole year behind?* Even so, I was certain that my year off had taught me more than one at my local university would have. Now here I was, about to head back to average college life.

"Section three now boarding." That was mine. As I took out my phone to turn it off for the flight, the "new e-mail message" icon illuminated.

"Monika, I am pleased to offer you a fall internship with the United States Congress," the message declared.

My jaw dropped open. I had applied to intern for Congressman Jared Polis in Washington, DC several weeks ago without knowing when his office would make their final decision. The news sent a rush of excitement over my body.

Now what? Do I study government at college or experience government firsthand? I began to pace the airport corridor. The dilemma seemed too easily solved. How could I possibly choose textbooks and theory over being where the magic is made? I'd be a much better student if I actually had firsthand knowledge and could contribute valuable insights to class discussions—although very few of my introductory classes would be available in the spring semester. That meant that I'd have to take a second year off to intern, just as I'd done the past year. Harvard Extension School would let me enroll in a class while abroad, so I wouldn't be losing an entire academic year and would still be mentally fresh when the time came for me to return to campus.

I arrived at the end of the corridor and paused to watch the airplanes sprint off into the horizon. *This internship could be another chance for me to really see if government is the right field for me*, I thought to myself. Maybe this would be my dream profession!

There was still so much world left to explore! Besides, serving my country by serving my congressman was too rare an opportunity to pass up. That concluded my college decision: I would work in DC while attending Harvard Extension School as a distance student.

After I boarded the airplane, I squeezed into the middle seat.

"Get ready, girl," the wrinkled woman next to me said while tilting the air conditioner toward her face. "This is gonna be a long ride."

And so began round two of my gap year.

CHAPTER THIRTEEN

Capitol Calling

Washington, DC

DC turns reality on its head. It's a business-card-switching, black-suit-donning, ladder-climbing hotspot controlled by twenty-four-year-olds paid in adrenalin. And yet the chance to say, "I was there," to be a part of history, creates an undeniable magnetic pull. The trick is to understand how the internal magnetic forces work—then to discover how to resist these forces' ability to destroy a healthy work-life balance.

Or so I would learn. Perhaps too late.

After my communications internships in New York, London, and San Francisco, I was drawn into the Capitol's magnetic force field in order to learn about government public relations.

Getting a job there had been the first hurdle. That required demonstrated dedication to my congressman, Jared Polis of Colorado, and a carefully crafted application. Having previously worked on the congressman's election campaign during high school, I knew about the district's most important issues from having gone door to door to encourage people to vote. I elaborated upon this experience as well as the impact I made while leading my high school student council. I also combined the completed application questions, a statement of interest and letters of recommendation with a cover page and table of contents in a neatly formatted PDF document. I'd submitted it before the deadline and kept in close contact with the office manager to show my continued interest.

The real work began after I was selected. I submersed myself in everything DC. My daily news reading quadrupled.

"Miss, there's a maximum of nine items that can be checked out at a time," the white-haired librarian told me. "So you'll have to come back for the other, um, twelve next week."

I checked out books on legislation, lobbying, political scandals, and touring the Capitol. I stocked my movie queue with documentaries, political satires, and political TV shows. If I didn't understand a joke or reference, I paused the media to research the hole in my understanding. As such, some episodes took me hours to finish. I'd never paused a show so many times as when I was preparing for Congress.

I set Google Alerts for Congressman Polis so I could receive all the relevant news, blogs, and web content related to him the moment they appeared. That way I'd know what was going on without searching to find it.

Next I researched the other Colorado representatives and senators, followed their tweets, and compiled a comprehensive list of reference materials that detailed the issues that mattered most to them. This would give me a broader understanding of Colorado's issues as a whole. Finally I interviewed past Congressional interns to discover which projects or opportunities during their internship they were most proud of. This taught me which opportunities to look out for (professional mentorships, capitol dome tours, and shadowing the congressman, for example) instead of relearning all the shortcuts.

My wardrobe was the easiest part to compile: pearl earrings, black silk pointed-toe high heels, and black-on-black-on-black everything else.

"Are you going to a funeral or to work for Congress?" my best friend, Bina, asked me over Skype as I packed my suitcase. "From the looks of your luggage, DC is where color and personal style go to die," she said with a laugh.

*   *   *

When my first week arrived, I settled into the duties of a typical Congressional intern—filing mail by issue area, reading relevant research reports, and answering phone calls.

"Hello again, Mr. Flins. What would you like to tell the congressman this morning?" I answered one day. Mr. Flins was among the population of homeless and unemployed who called daily. He practically made his new occupation "unofficial consultant to the congressman."

Thanks to callers such as Mr. Flins, my fellow interns and I knew better than anyone about the unemployment rate. All we had to do was count the number of "regulars" we talked to every day. If anyone wants people to get work, it's Congress, because they need their staffers to do research instead of answering phones all day.

"Uh-huh. Your neighbor is trying to control you with magnetic waves? I thought you said he stopped doing that yesterday. Oh. OK. He's doing it *again*. Yes, I'll let the congressman know. Thank you, Mr. Flins."

When I hung up the receiver, I went back to searching for an issue area where I could be most valuable. As I was interested in economics and finance, I wanted to become the office-intern specialist on these subjects. The only problem was that the position didn't exist. I set my mind to changing that.

For my proposal to work, I needed to take work off the full-time staffers while creating a valuable outcome. So I arranged for a short meeting to speak with the finance and tax staffer and proposed to annotate all the current legislation, Congressional Research Service reports, and newspapers for finance and tax-related subjects. Then I'd organize them for quick reference so she'd have everything she needed when the subject came to the floor. It took one seven-minute meeting to get the go-ahead.

I jumped right in. While I was swimming through financial legislation, the house minority leader apparently was scouting me.

On day ten of my internship, I was called into the congressman's office. The walls were painted a soothing faint yellow. Congressman Polis, among the youngest representatives in the House, sat reclined in his chair.

With his typical big smile, he began, "Monika, Leader Pelosi has been searching the entire Hill for two interns to serve on a special assignment she needs filled immediately. I recommended you a few days ago. Looks like you're among the finalists."

My eyes bulged. Me? I ran a mental list of the other seven interns in the office. They were law school students or seniors in college. I was by far the youngest and had the fewest days on the job. Wasn't I too inexperienced for such a prestigious opportunity? "Wow! That's...that's awesome! Thank you. I'm honored. But—"

A phone ring cut me off. Congressman Polis took the call and nodded at me. "Leader Pelosi's chief of staff would like to see you in the Capitol."

I ran so fast to get there that I can't even remember if he hung up the phone.

When I arrived, the secretary sitting inside the grand marble entryway smiled. "Welcome, Monika. Please take a seat in the conference room. The chief of staff is expecting you."

How did she know who I was? I wondered. I suppose nothing is secret at this level of government. I walked past her into the conference room.

At the front, a neoclassical fireplace sat beneath a nearly life-size portrait of Abraham Lincoln. A lavish crystal chandelier was suspended from the ceiling. As I looked around with my jaw unhinged, the reality of the situation set in. Was I actually prepared for this? I didn't have any time left to doubt myself.

A distinguished older man dressed in a tailored navy suit briskly entered the room. He shook my hand with confidence as two other staffers flanked him on both sides. The ladies sat nearly in unison beneath Lincoln's portrait, cracking manila folders and placing several documents before the gentleman— my résumé and a letter with the seal of the United States Congress were on the top.

"Monika," the man began, "we're looking for two interns to fulfill this special assignment. Are you interested in being one of them?"

Was that an offer? I was on guard for a grueling interview.

The gentleman must have sensed my train of thought and continued, "We've reviewed your personal background and professional history. Your congressman speaks very highly of you. Leader Pelosi would be very pleased if you would serve on this special assignment for her."

I came to Washington thinking I could earn my way by preparing the hardest and adding the most value to Congressman Polis's office. Yet in this moment, it seemed there was no fighting to be done, no hoops to jump through. One recommendation and the confirmation of the minority leader was all it took.

"If you agree, we can tell you just what it is you'll be doing."

Ask me to make a promise and then tell me what I'm promising? That sounded like my brother Norbert's way of tricking me into doing dishes when I lived at home. What if I was no good at the job?

I opened my mouth to insist on an explanation, but before I could, President Lincoln's overpowering gaze gripped me. The secretary who greeted me by name moved in my peripheral vision. The legislative branch of the United States of America's government was selecting me for a confidential position. If anyone knew how I could be of help and who I was, these were probably the people.

"At your service, sir." The line felt cheesy. In the moment, under that grand chandelier, with the sun streaming in off the Capitol lawn and Lincoln's watchful eyes looking firmly at mine, though, I did feel like I was serving my country.

The legal paperwork and briefings that came afterward solidified the seriousness of my work. Quickly I learned my position was a privilege—which is why twelve-hour days seemed like an honor. And why researching and sprinting to ensure every last aspect of the job was perfectly executed wasn't excruciating but "giving my best for my nation." Within these halls it was better to be seen working than heard. The opportunity to work personally with so many national leaders made it all worthwhile.

At the end of each workday, I scampered out of the Capitol and four blocks home to my all-girls' residence club, where a home-cooked dinner awaited me. As in San Francisco, two meals a day were included with my modest $925 rent. The house also had a gym, library, piano room, and rose garden, where I could work out, study, and unwind with the other girls at the end of each long day. Like most Congressional interns, I was unpaid, but since I had practically no external food costs, no transportation costs from walking to work, and enough cash left over from previous savings, my DC internship was all within my budget.

The best part of living in the residence club was the interaction with so many other female interns. At any dinner table, you could see a smattering of employers represented: Smithsonian, the Belgian embassy, the US Senate, Brookings Institution, Green Peace.

After dinner, during a regular late night one week, I opened my apartment door to see textbooks and flash cards piled feet high on my desk.

"Ugggh," I moaned, tossing my keys onto my bed and peeling off one high-heeled shoe after the other. I was enrolled in two classes as a distance student and needed to study for midterms, which were coming up in a week. My gym clothes hung over the closet door, reminding me of a desperately needed workout. The bedside clock read 8:37 p.m.

"Might as well keep going while I've got the adrenalin," I muttered, trying to pump myself up. My left hand grabbed my running shorts, my right a deck of flash cards and a textbook. Two flights of stairs later, I was in the downstairs library studying. When the clock gonged ten, I pushed in my headphones and took another flight of stairs down to the house gym.

My friends sat chatting on the couches in the adjoining room. "Flash cards on the elliptical again? Really, Monika, doesn't that give you motion sickness?"

I laughed, swinging myself onto the machine as I texted Bina. Work. Study. Fitness. Friends. I wasn't willing to sacrifice any aspect of my life.

*   *   *

By mid-November, I had crammed my way through midterm exams and was about to spend Thanksgiving in New Jersey with Bina. The absolute stress and upkeep of working, studying, and living were coming to a halt as I packed my bags.

I felt like I was jumping from one adrenalin burst to the next. Each day my schedule entailed studying before work, working, applying for summer internships during lunch, working more, running home, attending an educational event, studying, exercising, and calling friends and family while reviewing flash cards on the treadmill. At that point life felt like a treadmill, and I could barely control the speed.

Just get through the last day of work tomorrow and then you can take a break, I told myself as I stumbled over my luggage and into bed sometime after midnight. My eyes were so sore from studying and working that I couldn't even read my bedside clock.

The next morning, a buzzing alarm shocked me awake.

"Seriously?" I rubbed my sleep-swollen eyes and kicked a stack of freshly washed and neatly folded sheets off the foot of my bed. The truth was, I was so exhausted by the time I fell asleep that I couldn't care less if I slept on sheets or a bare mattress. Sleep was privilege enough.

With my eyes finally open, my body raised itself out of bed. Then collapsed.

I saw stars. I felt tingles race over my body. Then everything faded into numbness. I lay there for minutes. Dozens and dozens of minutes. As if I were in the last moments of consciousness before falling asleep, my mind ran through every motion and action I was supposed to take, but my body refused to listen. I had run it to the very last drop, and now, without the constant push toward midterms or work, it quit.

It took all my energy to grasp my cell phone, which lay just inches away from my head. "Eric," I texted my colleague, "feeling a little under the weather. Will be an hour late for work. Plz tell Leader." I hit "Send" and slumped back onto the floor.

Eliza, my usual breakfast companion, knocked at the door. "Mon, are you coming to breakfast?"

"It's, it's open..." My voice was faint.

Eliza gingerly pushed open the door until she saw me lying on the floor. "Monika!" She rushed in and dropped to her knees besides me. "Are you...? What the...? What's going on?" Worriedly, her eyes scanned my face; she touched my forehand then reached for my pulse. "You pushed it too far, Monika" She shook her head.

My phone buzzed. I struggled to reach it.

Eliza stopped me, "No, Mon. You can't keep doing this. The on-the-go partial meals. The insane schedule. The lack of sleep. No. You have to go to the hospital."

I summoned some energy to reply. "No. No problem. Just a...just..." The stars came back and I forgot what I was talking about.

The next thing I knew, my colleagues were texting me, calling me, and asking to help. The day was a series of blurred hours. Some spent asleep. Some spent awake. All with minimal awareness. Since my grandfather was a medical doctor, I called him from bed, dizzy and coughing, to describe my symptoms.

"Sounds like you've worn yourself down and caught a case of strep throat in the process." His diagnosis startled me.

Food and sleep, I told myself. *That'll fix this.* When I finally stumbled downstairs to eat that evening, my friends stopped me at the table.

"Rachel is getting a cab, Monika. The three of us are taking you to the hospital." Eliza spoke forcefully, but I knew it was because she cared.

I started to shake my head, but the movement made me dizzy. I toppled into a chair to regain my strength. The girls nearly carried me into the car.

When I reopened my eyes, I was in a hospital bed at George Washington University.

Now what?

I saw the needle pricks in my fingers and the turquoise hospital band around my wrist. How did this happen? I shook my head. Lately I'd been feeling weak with fatigue, but instead of sleeping or resting, I had drunk black tea. Straight. If one cup didn't work, I'd make a second, third, fourth. Whatever it took to get me through the task at hand. How could I think it wouldn't catch up with me?

I thought I'd left my high school habits of burnout behind. I was wrong. The person I'd been in high school could only go away if I stopped acting like her. Maybe I was just afraid to say, "no." I was afraid I couldn't be less than everything to everyone: my colleagues, professors, and friends. Now which was worse—admitting my humanity and maybe disappointing someone or lying helpless in an emergency room bed?

I knew exactly whom to blame for my collapse—myself. It wasn't class; I loved what I was studying. It wasn't Congress; I truly felt honored to uphold my position there. All these things were possible in combination, but I had to treat them that way—as percentages in the 100 percent of my life, not 100 percent each.

Me, Monika. *I* was the one who piled one item after another onto my shoulders. It wasn't my dedication to exercise or being social either. The relationships I fostered were the reason I was even at the hospital at all.

Why hadn't I stopped to ask what this was all worth to me? What was the worth of a high-profile internship if I never made it home to eat with my friends? What was a 4.0 worth if it cost me my health? And when was enough finally enough? Now, apparently. This was too much of a scare to live through without learning from it. At that moment I realized that the imaginary line between "living life to the fullest" and "overextending yourself" really does exist—and has serious consequences when ignored.

Throughout the night, my housemates Rachel and Abbie came in and checked on me. Lying weak on that bed, I realized it wasn't a shiny internship or great grades that fulfilled me. Rather it was great friends and caring colleagues that made the difference in my life.

In that hospital bed, I realized my limits, my weaknesses, and, above all, my need to define my priorities. I needed to stack my chips on only a few aspects of my life, or else risk spreading myself thin and enduring another episode of watching the House wipe me clean.

This was one form of personal education that life taught me. Adaptability was next on the syllabus. Singapore would be my professor.

CHAPTER FOURTEEN

Trouble in Paradise

Singapore, Singapore

There's no place like home for the holidays. Nestled back in the Rocky Mountains for Christmas, I was more appreciative than ever of family and home. Aware that I was headed to Singapore for my next internship, I didn't even mind the Colorado snow.

One e-mail, however, brought the entire joy ride to a screeching halt.

"Chirp. Chirp," my Blackberry sang. I toggled the screen with my pinky as I continued to eat breakfast with my dad.

"New e-mail from: Yasmine [the internship coordinator at my upcoming job]."

> *Hi, Monika. Just checked your visa status. Looks like it got rejected again. Not sure what we can do from here, but I'll keep working on it. Have a merry Christmas!*

I dropped my oatmeal spoon and looked at my dad. "Rejected again? Is this happening? This is the fourth time! I thought everything already had been worked out! I'm already packed to leave!"

I set the phone down on the table and continued my outburst. "I can't stay in Singapore for four months without a job! Besides, I already paid for my housing deposit, first month's rent, and plane tickets. Now what?"

Sighing, Dad rubbed the temples of his forehead out of frustration. "Well, Monika, I think American tourists can stay in Singapore for two months at least. Why don't you go there as a tourist and appeal to the immigration office for your work visa? After it gets confirmed, start going to work."

I was pacing the kitchen like a cooped up zoo animal.

"What if that doesn't work? I mean, I picked Singapore because I wanted to explore the country and study Mandarin." I paused and looked out the snow-frosted window. "And it's *warm* there."

Dad tugged at his three-layers of sweaters and laughed in agreement.

"OK. What can I do there while my visa gets processed? Take some Mandarin classes to get school credit? That would be worth it." I paused to give Dad his chance to respond.

"Well, if warmth, Mandarin, and travel are what you want to do, and you can support yourself, go for it. If things change, adapt. If you really want something and you're willing to adapt, things will always work out. Just stop pacing."

I stood still.

"All right then. Cut your internship to two months," Dad continued. "And why don't you go back to the companies you turned down before, say your situation has changed, and that you can still start in April or so?"

I nodded slowly as I processed the idea. "Yeah. OK. I guess I'm off to send follow-up e-mails!" I pushed my dirty oatmeal bowl next to Norbert. "Thanks for cleaning up!" I hollered at him over my shoulder. Having a time crunch was the perfect excuse to make my brother do the dishes.

I needed to make sure the other companies I had turned down in favor of Singapore knew that I was still interested before they made their final spring hiring decisions.

*   *   *

WELCOME TO SINGAPORE! a smiling, animated immigration poster beamed at me. I rubbed my sleep-swollen eyes to make sure I was reading it correctly.

Getting to this point was an accomplishment. I checked the date on my phone. Two days and three flights had come and gone since I'd boarded that first plane in Denver. *Singapore must be a paradise*, I joked to myself while waiting in the immigration line, *because getting here sure was hell.*

Hungry, I zipped open my second carry-on bag, a tan oversize handbag. Learning from my London debacle, it served as my emergency pack in case I missed a flight or had to endure another airport detainment scene. I dug around my phone and laptop chargers (plus their converters), about fifty US dollars in local currency, contact lens solution, a sleeping mask, melatonin (for avoiding jet lag), and dried snacks. The snacks sounded amazing right now. I rummaged deeper to find two copies of my travel documents—one in paper and another stored in the "cloud" so I could access it from anywhere with Wi-Fi. The contact number for the American embassy and printed turn-by-turn directions to my hostel (including bus and subway routes, just in case) were also included in my carry-on and online storage.

Popping a dried mango into my mouth, I took a taxi to my new home, a modest youth hostel. Even as a paid intern, finding housing within my budget was a challenge. Fortunately a hostel located outside of downtown for foreign students had posted an opening online. Although I would have preferred to live with locals instead of other foreigners, being surrounded by other students my age would make building a community much easier.

An hour into the ride, I became a bit skeptical of the journey.

"Um, excuse me, sir," I said to the driver. "Mapquest says my hostel is only twenty miles from the airport." I poked the turn-by-turn directions over his shoulder. "I heard it only takes forty-five minutes to drive the entire island of Singapore. We've been driving for an hour. Are you sure we're going to the right place?"

The Malaysian man smiled at me through yellowed teeth. "No traffic, forty-five minutes." He laughed. "But Singapore always have traffic. Lots ah traffic." He chuckled a raspy, cigarette-worn laugh and turned back to the wheel.

I sunk into my seat and watched the palm trees crawl past my window until we finally arrived.

At check-in I realized that in Singapore it actually is possible to live in paradise—on a tropical island, with amazing food, incredibly diverse culture, and world-leading businesses. The only caveat was that paradise came with a heap of rules.

This I learned from the hostel's contract for residents:

- *You can only access the laundry machines during certain hours and must use specific laundry cards to do so.*
- *The basketball and tennis courts must be reserved a minimum of one day in advance. The prices change depending on the hour and day of the week.*
- *This is a list of all the foods that may not be consumed in the public gardens...*

Perhaps in Singapore more rules equals more safety, I thought. *More safety means more happiness.* And everyone wanted to be as happy as the animated icons that adorned the public spaces.

After a squabble over the preagreed terms of my contract that weren't updated on the current form, the secretary grabbed a set of keys off the desk. "This way, please," she said, ushering me to my room.

Down winding hallways adorned in pastel hues and across a palm-framed courtyard, she led me to my new home. Swinging open the door, I saw a single room in front of me with three beds, three desks, and one window. The middle bed was stripped bare. The secretary pointed to it while retreating back towards the door. "This is yours. Please remember that random checks for cleanliness and adherence to residence standards will be conducted."

I dropped my bags and looked across the room in one sweeping glance. When I turned back, the door slammed and I was suddenly alone.

Alone. And lonely. The feeling lingered for four days. Thinking that the long holiday would give me time to overcome any jetlag and get acquainted with the island before I started work, I'd checked in on the eve of the Chinese New Year holiday. Unfortunately for me, everything was closed, and all the usual residents were out. I tried hanging around in the common areas, but my attempts to meet people in passing were in vain.

Now what? I was homesick. *Maybe I'll try reaching out to friends*, I thought. But the extreme time difference forced me to cherish e-mails received the moment I awoke. No more would come all day.

I tried distracting myself until my first day of work by studying Chinese out of a personal desire to learn. I tried studying in my room, but the air was stuffy and mold ridden. There was so much humidity that when I left my closet locked over the weekend, my suits were speckled with pea-size white growths on Monday morning.

I went outside for runs. Then I returned to studying under the palm trees until I was too hungry to focus. At that point I'd make dinner out of a cup of ramen noodles because the restaurants and grocery stores nearby were closed. There was little left to do then but study late into the night. Soon I'd fall asleep listening to Frank Sinatra songs on YouTube and wake up the next morning to start my habit again.

Sick of studying and running, I was overtaken by loneliness one morning. I decided to e-mail the Cru National Missions director, whom I'd met at a conference the year before.

"Mr. Dishman," I began, "so far I've found literal sunshine in Singapore but no one to help bring light into my life. Is there a Cru here that you could help me find?"

Quickly the e-mail was tossed around the globe, and within a day, an invitation appeared in my inbox. "Monika, please meet Audrey, a student member of Cru at Singapore Management University. Her group is pleased to invite you in."

"Have you been alone this whole time?" Audrey asked me that night over the phone.

"Oh, no!" I half laughed, leaning back in my desk chair. "I've had the company of..." I glanced at the pile of textbooks I was annotating at my desk. "...of books and uh..." Then I nodded quietly. "Uh, yeah, it's been just me."

"Want to meet tomorrow?" she replied.

"Yes!" I blurted. My eagerness to spend time with anything besides my textbooks was difficult to disguise.

The next thing I knew, I was in a high-tech classroom listening to testimonies of former Chinese students who had left the People's Republic of China for school in Singapore and found Christ in the process. Growing up in a Catholic home, I'd never met so many people who had just discovered the Bible. In that book they found truths about themselves that their previous government forbade them to discover. Now in Singapore, they were free to discuss, question, and learn. Their zeal and curiosity were contagious!

To my surprise they jumped to invite me to dinners or Bible studies, despite my being a foreigner. I loved teaching them about American culture and learning "Singlish" (a slang Singaporean dialect that's a rough combination of Mandarin Chinese grammar and English words). They cooked for me, toured me around the island, and eagerly introduced me to new foods.

From them I learned that Singaporeans refer to shopping and eating as their national pastimes. *Laksa. Poh pia.* Bubble tea. Carrot cake (which contains no actual carrots, I discovered). And chicken rice. These were just the beginning of a very slippery slope of foodie-ism I fell down in my first two weeks on the island. In those fourteen days, I sampled them all, plus stingray, chicken feet, and fish eyes.

"Try this one! Try this one!" A girl passed a plastic plate piled with exotic appetizers my way. When I gleefully accepted, the entire table seemed to shrink as each head leaned in to watch my reaction.

"Mmm! Ah! Hot! Hot!" I fanned my mouth and jolted out of my seat for a glass of water. The whole table erupted in high-pitched giggles.

Of course the sampling wasn't all fun and games. My new friends did put me through "the durian test"—a standard recruitment procedure for any foreigner looking to fit in with a group of locals. Durian, a local fruit delicacy, emits such a pungent stench that it's illegal to eat it in airports and on public transportation. It smelled like hot trash left in the sweltering New York heat on a late-summer afternoon. It's an acquired taste, enjoyed mostly by locals. After force-swallowing a tiny portion, I learned the key to passing the test is not to *enjoy* the fruit. You just have to stomach it.

The real tests began when my internship with FutureBrand, an international brand consulting firm, started the next day.

I practiced my commute that evening to ensure that I wouldn't get lost on day one. I took note of everything around me. Shopping malls on every corner. Maseratis prowling over perfectly kept roadways. And some of the lowest crime rates in the world. Twice in one day, I saw backpacks abandoned under palm trees that were still untouched by the time I past them again that night.

Feeling safe gave me the emotional energy to dedicate myself to my work. In the first week, I was assigned to three accounts, including a major food label (similar to Hershey's), an influential bank (similar to HSBC), and an international university. The opportunity to have my voice heard on projects, get my hands dirty, and present with the team made my work very rewarding.

Although hardworking, the environment in the office was uplifting and friendly. My team comprised ten people from nine nationalities. Getting along with each one wasn't particularly difficult but certainly required cultural sensitivity. My direct supervisor, Rob, and I were both Americans, so we bonded over not using "u"s when the team would discuss "colour schemes" or "labour contracts." Lav, a Saudi Arabian educated at Northwestern, laughed along with us.

At the start of each new project, our consulting team would all pile into a whiteboard-walled room stocked with couches and overflowing candy dishes. There we would draw. We would imagine. We would build off one another's ideas. It was where brands were born. It was the environment where "Live the Coke life," "Mmm, mmm, good," and "Just do it" probably originated. It was like cooking mind popcorn; ideas just popped in and out of the air.

I felt equal among my peers and cared for as an individual. They treated me like a protégé or friendly coworker but never as a rented intern. Lav and I took weekend trips to Thailand together. Rob wrote me an itinerary of his favorite local highlights in Kuala Lumpur. The entire office even took me on a bus to the coast to introduce me to a local spice-covered seafood favorite—chili crab.

Granted, it was a long road to earning that desk. FutureBrand was part of the same family corporation as the marketing company I'd worked for in Shanghai and the communications firm I'd worked for in New York. From my strong recommendations at those two companies, I was internally recommended to the brand-strategy firm in Singapore. It took multiple difficult interviews before I got an offer. I'd also overcome four visa rejections.

My days were long and challenging. In order to arrive around seven every morning, I had to leave my hostel at 5:47 a.m. Since housing was so expensive, I could only afford to live farther away from downtown. This forced me to choose between sleeping an extra hour and spending two hours in traffic or dragging myself out of bed before sunrise and working on the bus during a mere forty-five-minute trip to my office. I chose the latter. I figured it was better to leave earlier, study on the bus, and get to work early enough to get a head start on the day's projects than waste two hours in traffic every morning.

Working with my team for such distinguished clients as international food conglomerates and famous bank CEOs filled me with constant energy. My parents used to tell me, "When you're aligned with your passion, you will never lack energy." I had spent the past eighteen months trying out careers I thought I wanted only to realize that the action of traveling around and having to quickly learn the ins and outs of new industries and teams was what I loved. The more I worked alongside my team, the more I realized how much I would enjoy a consulting job like this post graduation. After checking off "social entrepreneurship" and "fashion design," I finally had narrowed myself down to a career I loved.

On a late, long bus ride home after work, I watched a group of Western tourists ogle each famous landmark we passed. *Why aren't I as excited as they are?* I wondered. I already had explored every urban and natural jungle in Singapore. Maybe I needed to get off the island to reignite that awe. After all I should do more in Singapore than just intern and eat.

From the upper deck of that cherry-red Singaporean shuttle, I started to devise a new plan.

CHAPTER FIFTEEN

World-Class Education

Kuala Lumpur, Malaysia

"Ouch. Ouch. Oooooh." I painstakingly slid into my office chair, exhaling with relief when I finally touched the base.

Lav, seated at the desk next to me, smiled knowingly at my awkward self-conduct. "Sunburned, again?" She passed me the bottle of aloe vera that was just out of my arm's reach. I eagerly accepted it. "Where were you this time?"

"Bali." I smiled back, attempting to ignore my discomfort.

"Alone?" She looked concerned.

"No, funny story actually. I met a local Singaporean in DC last year. He was an exchange student at the George Washington University. When I got to Singapore, he offered to introduce me to a couple of his friends. One happens to be Mia, the owner and designer for the fashion brand Emblem, who does her production in Bali. I'd never been to Indonesia, so she offered to show me around the island. My gosh, she knew everybody there! Ouch." I squirted more aloe vera on my shin and rubbed it in.

My travel partners these days were colleagues, immediate friends from America, or their friends. The more people I told in the United States about my being in Singapore, the more they introduced me to classmates, colleagues, and family abroad who graciously offered to host or travel with me because I was alone abroad.

"Where are you going this weekend?" Lav took a sip of her fragrant black tea.

"Well, since we already did Thailand last week, I booked a trip to Kuala Lumpur."

My busy travel schedule was part of my attempt at "experiential" education. Instead of learning about other countries through the news and books, I wanted to explore their realities in person and through the locals' perspective. In addition to advanced travel tricks, these journeys taught me political and cultural education not printed in newspapers but plastered over the hearts and minds of their citizens.

The experiment was possible because I had negotiated four-day workweeks at the beginning of my internship agreement. Since airfare and accommodations in the region were so inexpensive, I had more to gain by traveling than what I could do with the money I'd make by working a fifth day. Surprisingly the reduced workweek changed the type of work I did at the office. Since I had fewer hours, my team gave me important projects they most needed help with instead of time-filling "intern work."

Monday through Thursday, I did my class homework on the approximately one-hour commute to the office, worked intensively during the day, studied on the way home, then jogged, packed, and met friends in the evenings. Friday through Sunday I spent abroad. The system forced me to be efficient with my time. For instance I'd listen to my Chinese audio tracks while running to an outdoor public cafeteria called Hawker Centers for dinner with friends. In the two hours that the outing would take me, I'd listen to an hour of Chinese, exercise for two thirty-minute running cycles, eat dinner, and spend time with friends—a balance I really enjoyed.

I thought all the constant movement would exhaust me. To my surprise, I slept better at night because I worked so hard during the days and I got up easier in the mornings because I knew I had things to get done. I spent my weekends unwinding, so when I got back to work afterward, I felt refreshed.

Every time I traveled, however, something unexpected popped up—meaning, every time I traveled, I learned a new lesson in planning, organization, and safety. In Bali, for instance, I learned to call my credit card company before traveling so they wouldn't decline my card when I made a charge in another country. Again. I learned to count the bills I received at the money exchange shop after they handed me the envelope to ensure they didn't drop a bill on the floor while stuffing it for me. Again.

Thailand was a lesson in backup travel procedures and how to plan for them. I took pictures of my flight confirmation and saved them in my phone in case I lost my Wi-Fi connection. Then I had the digital confirmation sent to my phone two hours before my flight by using the "delayed send" function on my e-mail account. I kept two printouts of my itinerary: one for my notebook, which I keep physically on me at all times, and the second inside my luggage. That way I could afford to lose a copy, and if my luggage got lost, the crew would find my itinerary when they opened my bag and know where to send it. Most important, I stored digital copies of my visa and passport in a separate "cloud" in case I was robbed and needed to get back into Singapore or the United States.

By far I learned the most in Malaysia. When I touched down in Kuala Lumpur, I didn't know what my host looked like. I also didn't have a plan for how to get to a hotel if I needed one. After wandering through the airport terminal once, I figured it was best not to ask anyone if they were my host or were looking for me. It would be too easy for a person with bad intentions to simply agree and get me to come along. I waited for someone to approach me first.

At the first doorway, a well-groomed woman stood calmly. I walked near her but out of arm's reach. Before I could even open my mouth, she smiled knowingly. "This way, Monika," she said.

Out of instinct, I put a pointed finger to my chest, as if to clarify that I was the Monika she was looking for. She laughed and extended her hand to take my one piece of luggage.

"But how did you know—" I started to ask curiously.

"You're the only natural blonde who's walked through the terminal all hour." She smiled again. "You're harder to miss than you think."

Darn. In all my time living in Asia, I constantly forgot that I didn't blend in. I guess in some cases it was an advantage.

Between skyscrapers that shot up like stalagmites and late-night street-cart snacks in alleyways, my Malaysian hosts taught me football (meaning soccer) diplomacy. Before I started talking about Arsenal, I was invisible. Once I did, my host's son said, "You're an Arsenal fan from abroad? That makes you family!"

During extended meal times over local *idli* snacks, they explained local myths, national rivalries, and honest insights into how their government's corruption was hindering the lives of the lowest classes. The family was moving the country forward with their organization, EPIC Collaborative, which changed people's lives at the lowest levels of development by building them homes. Their excitement was inspirational, their humility unbreakable. I didn't feel the need to be composed or to have everything figured out. Simply, all I needed was a positive attitude, an open mind, and the desire to learn from them.

Football diplomacy. Food diplomacy. Faith. There are enough documentaries and papers on these topics to fill a suitcase. But unlike reading textbooks or watching YouTube videos, I'd never forget what I'd learned in my weekend travels because I *experienced* it. In these journeys, I was reminded that the world and its people have more to teach me than any book or internship could. There are precious experiences that have no place on a résumé and bundles of insights worthy of recollection, even if they never show up on an exam.

During these journeys, I saw that schools promise us education, not wisdom. Outcomes, not understanding. I saw that it's possible to have a world-class education that doesn't come with a diploma or a $200,000 price tag. These types of lessons are priceless.

I taped a picture of my new Malaysian family on my hostel desk back in Singapore. Their tan skin, shiny black hair, and glittery smiles illuminated the corner. "Best looking diploma I've ever seen," I said with a grin.

CHAPTER SIXTEEN

Captain of My Own (Intern)Ship

Washington, DC

Twenty hours of plane travel later, I rolled my bag out of Reagan National Airport and onto the tongue of a slender crimson carpet. Its teeth—opulent crystal chandeliers—lit my way down the velvety trail.

Do I actually get to work here? I asked myself. After six interviews spent illustrating my endorsement of Omni Hotel's company values, my background in luxury hotel marketing from New York City, and experience serving congressmen on the Hill, I still couldn't believe I was offered a customized paid position in the historic DC hotel. I tried not to look around for fear of being labeled a star-struck intern on my first day. During my next four months as a management-strategy intern, this grand hotel would be my office.

Every week I rotated to a different division in the hotel (HR, accounting, convention services, sales, front desk, select guest, et cetera) then reported back to the general manager to discuss which opportunities for collaboration or improvements I discovered. Admittedly, an award-winning, four-diamond hotel wasn't the easiest place to find problems. Nonetheless, during my initial hotel tour, I spotted my opportunity—the hotel's laundry.

The Omni Shoreham's laundry room is a cavern of roof-scraping machines and linen piles. Narrow patches of cloth-free ground designated a pathway through the heaps. Despite the mounds of metal and cloth, the air was thick with the smell of flowers.

I inhaled deeply with delight. "Mmmm, laundry-detergent scent."

"Andrew," I said, calling to the laundry manager. His midtwenties face poked out of his office on the other side of the terrycloth mountain range. "What's our protocol for recycling linens we don't use anymore?"

"Well," he said, as he dodged a cart of folded bedsheets, "besides making them into rags, none."

I raised my eyebrows. Regular hires probably overlooked this as standard operating procedure, but from my out-of-industry eyes, it seemed like an ideal area for improvement.

"Mind if I borrow a few?" I asked, picking up a fluffy former pool towel.

I rushed back to my desk with starry eyes. After completing so many other internships, I was looking for an opportunity to find my own way to add value to an organization. I needed something that didn't exist before me, didn't add anything more than supervisory work to others' plates, and could continue after my departure.

First I needed to know how big our problem actually was. If we had only fifty discards a year, management wouldn't pay attention to it. I went back to Andrew to get more accurate details. The more numbers I had, the more likely the administration would be willing to listen to my proposal. Then I went through the ordering manager to find out how much each item cost us. I needed a dollar amount for the discards to illustrate the value a recycling program could bring.

So what's my program? I asked myself in my office. I stared at the hump of linen on my desk. Towels. Sheets. Pillowcases. They all had small tears or light stains from customer use.

Homeless shelter donations? No, they wouldn't want torn linens.

Fort-building competitions in the lobby? No, not classy enough for our clientele.

A pillowcase decorating project for children? I could imagine the paint on our velvet carpet...

I needed something that staff members could value and stand behind. I'd need the support of each division if the executives were going to let me put a program into operation.

I looked on Pinterest.com for craft ideas with pillowcases

and towels. An Alaskan Malamute dog gnawing at a braided chew toy reminded me of Sonic.

"Dog toys!" I exclaimed. "Dogs don't care about tears or stains!" I pulled out a pair of scissors and started to make a prototype to show my boss.

"The head of catering loves dogs," I said aloud. "I'll bring her two for her black Labs to try out. Elizabeth in sales and her boyfriend just got a puppy. Everyone in the hotel is already in love with him. I'll give her a few prototypes and ask her to take pictures, and I'll use them in my presentation to the general manager. That would bring the project close to home."

As the weeks went on, I worked on the project in my free time and gained support across the hotel's divisions. The final outcome was a community volunteer day hosted on premise. I coordinated with Humane Societies and local community groups to bring in toy-making volunteers and give their shelters the finished products.

The day after the event, I walked through the laundry room to get the final toy count. I almost didn't recognize the place. The ever-present linen divide was gone.

Andrew laughed at my surprised expression, "Yep, you used them all up. Probably topped three hundred toys, I'd say."

My eyes lit up. "That's enough to stock the Humane Society shelters in DC, Virginia, and Maryland for the rest of the year!"

"Then it looks like DC, Virginia, and Maryland shelter animals are going to have a good year," he said with a smile, as he pointed to the hallway that was filled with bagged toys.

I beamed. It took the support of every hotel division and the trust of the general manager to make the program a reality. The achievement said less about my skills and more about Omni's willingness to listen to input from employees at every level. It felt awesome to work for a company that desired to make changes that bettered the community.

Wading through laundry-fresh dog toys in that cement hallway, I realized I had come to Omni to see the inner workings of operations but had stayed to learn from the general manager,

Pete Sams. Patient, intelligent, and full of energy, he has a way of making you feel like the only person in a crowded room. His ability to hear what people mean (even when they don't say it) and desire to be present for employees of every rank make him stand out immediately. In Pete I found a leadership role model. Interacting with him every day taught me that an internship doesn't have to be about the hard skills; one spent learning leadership or management talents is equally valuable.

Before leaving the laundry room, I snapped a picture of an old towel next to a new dog toy. The towel hung limp. Its stains were visibly noticeable. The toy, however, stood upright displaying its intricate twist of turquoise and white linens. Looking at the contrast, I smiled. *That's the difference that coming together with a vision can make in the world*, I told myself.

CHAPTER SEVENTEEN

Must Be This Old to Intern

Washington, DC

Three sunrises after my final day at the Omni Shoreham, I found myself surrounded by fellow interns under the flapping of a European flag.

"Who's up for a post-work drink?" my fellow intern called out. The group roared in approval. "This way, then."

The herd crossed the street, leaving me abandoned on the curb. At twenty years old, I wasn't even old enough to go out with the other *interns*. Sheepishly I rubbed my high-heeled shoes against the curb's chiseled surface. "Child, party of one," I mocked myself under my breath.

Clearly my life on the economics and finance desk of a European embassy wasn't what I'd expected it to be. Here I was, a dwarf among giants compared to the other interns, just as the seams of the euro were bursting. Every newspaper I picked up seemed to be shouting at me. *The Economist* was practically a review of my past five days at the office. Every day felt like a series of adrenalin bursts as news broke and delegates interacted. It was a lot to take in.

Maybe the internship would have been less overwhelming if, on my second day on the job, I hadn't casually asked my boss about next semester's intern talent pool while she was sifting through their applications. "Anything stand out?" I'd said.

"Oh, yeah," she said, mid-reach to her tea-stained mug. "All the sophomores in college who think they're prepared enough to handle the work we do. We need people who can think and write at a higher level, you know?" Her powder-blue eyes locked on mine, awaiting confirmation.

I froze. I hadn't even finished my freshman year of classes yet. Was that a hint that I wasn't meeting expectations? I felt serious pressure to live up to the standards of the other interns. Practically every one had an undergraduate degree and some or all of a master's degree already. After all, our work didn't stop at our desks. It would eventually go on to decision makers in Europe who would lean on it for insight. Should I have waited to intern here until I was a junior or postgrad like everyone else? I shook my head to silence the maddening thoughts and returned to reality. I was still standing in my boss's office.

I nodded quickly. "Uh, yes. Well, speaking of higher-level work, I'll return to these briefing pages and get them back to you by this evening before close of business." I spun around so fast that I nearly blew the applications off her desk.

In the protected solitude that only elevators seem to provide, I began to think out loud. "Did I just slip through the cracks? Couldn't be," I reassured myself. I'd spent months attending embassy events, interviewing former interns, and making coffee meetings with a senior staff member before I even had submitted my application. For the coffee chat alone, I took the effort to research the types of situations the embassy staff was dealing with and which skills and knowledge bases the best interns had.

My perfect IB Economics test score and grades proved I was capable of doing the job. Besides, the work I did as the economics and finance intern at Congress the year before provided me with the industry knowledge this embassy needed. In total it was nearly a three-month courting process.

All right, I thought, *even if I am the youngest, I can't let my work show it. I'll produce extra drafts, incorporate feedback, and always deliver the final report in advance for review so I can make any changes before the actual deadline. That should protect me against messing up. As time goes by, I'll get into the swing of things and will require less feedback.*

To do that, I needed to be on top of what was going on in the intersection of politics and macroeconomics. With the euro crashing, that wasn't a small task. It seemed like I could never learn fast enough. Since doing research and writing reports were at the center of my job, local finance events and lectures became a vital part of my research. The more events I went to, the more I understood where certain institutions stood on various subjects, who the thought leaders were, and where the rivalries flared. The fastest way to get a foothold was to attend lectures and discussions, Google the presenters, and listen to question-and-answer sessions. That's how I could tell where the hot spots of a topic were.

Somewhere between the piles of annotated economic indicators on my desk and sprints to think-tank discussions, it hit me; my age didn't prevent me from keeping up with my work. Who said I "must be this old" to start exploring my career? And why would I spend years contemplating my academic major when I could start figuring it out now? Just because I couldn't go to happy hours with my colleagues didn't mean I couldn't find happiness in my current position.

Actually I had several unspoken advantages over my more senior interns. First, I could walk away. I hadn't dedicated my entire academic career to get here. I didn't have to struggle through a degree in economics. I didn't need a job offer to maintain my current lifestyle. In fact I was blessed to get another room in my old residence club where my earnings from working at the hotel paid my way for the semester.

Second, I was learning more than everyone else because I didn't already know everything. When I went on my gap year, some members of my family thought that I'd never go back to school. Now I *wanted* to learn. Every day of learning and interacting with the world's financial thought leaders—from ambassadors to US Treasury executives—was an incredible opportunity that made me hungry for more knowledge to do my job. Most days I self-taught myself finance to understand what was going on. I needed to really understand—not for a test but for *me*. That was the strongest motivating force I'd ever encountered.

When I handed my end-of-the-month report to my boss one morning, she smiled at the work. "Well done, Monika. Why don't we go to tea to celebrate?"

"Celebrate finishing the report?" I asked, confused.

"No, celebrate your last week on internship." She leaned over her report-littered desk to the European monthly calendar on her wall. Pointing at the date, she turned her slender face back toward me, "Don't you head to Cambridge this weekend?"

I'd been so caught up in all the activity and learning that I'd nearly forgotten I was moving to college that week. Six swipes of a security badge later, I was standing on the street curb.

In my black-on-black suit and French braided hair, I admired the flapping of the embassy's flag one final time. Its rolling fabric fingers waved good-bye to me in the wind.

My internship was over. More startlingly, so was my second gap year. *I'm just a student now*, I thought. *I'm going to college tomorrow. My only job is to learn, to absorb, to produce work for the sake of practice. I don't have to solve immediate problems or influence someone's actions, except maybe a grader's. The next year of my life is well paved from here on out!*

I studied the edge of the curb beneath me for a few seconds then crossed the street. There a crowd of people was bustling their way down the block. I matched their stride. And blended in.

CHAPTER EIGHTEEN

Full Circle and Pay-Off

Cambridge, Massachusetts

"And to those of you from Boston, welcome home." The fluttering blonde flight attendant aboard Flight 771 from Washington, DC, was the first woman to welcome me to college life.

"Ya fram heah too?" The mid-fifties Bostonian in a Red Sox baseball cap asked me as he looked out my plane window at the pouring rain. I smelled the faint hint of Dunkin' Donuts coffee on his breath.

"Um, I'm about to be," I replied slowly. Reality had barely settled in. Tomorrow I would take my first in-person class at Harvard. Now what?

I closed my eyes in the airplane seat and remembered April 1, 2010. That day showed me that *I* was April's fool. Up until that day, I had fabricated a world outlook that told me happiness and success could fit inside one large manila envelope—where a small committee's one-word answer could decide one's future and worth.

"No."

That one word changed my life.

I waited inside the stuffy plane and reflected on the past two years. Every "Now what?" had brought me face to face with challenges that had prepared me for life, academics, and career. Each of the eleven companies, nine cities, six countries, and forty-seven airplane flights had brought me closer to the person I am today.

Without Nepal and India, I wouldn't have realized that success is contextual and that thinking I want to do something isn't enough to make me prepared for (or good at) it. San Francisco showed me that people skills are as vital as know-how.

Yosemite and the meditation retreat proved that spiritual enrichment shouldn't be neglected in the search for college and career. If not for London I couldn't have known what it feels like to pursue something with every ounce of energy, intellect, and force that I can. Before New York I didn't pay attention to personal safety, the importance of a nourishing work environment, or how full-hearted determination and prayer can make the unlikely happen in a matter of days.

China showed me that glitz isn't enough to make a job fulfilling and that ignoring toxic relationships actually can enflame them. Until Singapore I hadn't discovered that adaptability and community can mean the difference between paradise and depression. From Kuala Lumpur and Vietnam, I realized that experiences with no résumé value can still carry great life value.

Luck comes to those who prepare—and those who are willing to take risks, I learned in DC. Outside the Capitol, the city taught me the consequences of a balance-less life. Moreover it illustrated that age doesn't determine how much value I can add to a firm, and being the youngest intern often comes with the fewest chains and the most rewards.

"Ladies and gentlemen, please do not stand up in your seats." The flight attendant's silky voice was laced with frustration now. "You will *all* disembark from the plane. There is no need to move for the sake of moving."

I smiled at the metaphor her statement seemed to make about my choice to delay college. If I had come straight from high school to this moment, I would have been a different person entirely. Back then I'd wanted to go to an Ivy League school because I thought it meant I was special. It meant I'd been chosen from the crowd to be among the best educated in the world.

Now I didn't feel superior in any way. Now I saw that Harvard didn't save me from detainment in London or protect me from stalkers in New York City. Furthermore I had earned every internship over the past two years *without* being a Harvard grad. Most importantly, I realized I was still capable of being loved and appreciated even if I hadn't come from a world-famous academic institution.

"The captain has turned off the fastened-seatbelt sign. You are now free to move about the cabin," the flight attendant sang out. I watched as the other passengers scrambled to grab their luggage; I was in no such hurry.

After my gap years, I didn't feel like I "deserved" to be at Harvard. I felt like the same Monika, with all my inferiorities and ambitions, who had been rejected from college two years before. I realized the college years of my life wouldn't be the zenith of my existence. Rather they simply would be another steppingstone in my life path.

*   *   *

"What about *real* college life, Monika? What about partying and being a kid?" my new friends on campus asked me.

Admittedly, going directly into the professional world from high school did make me feel like I'd missed the opportunity to be a regular college kid. I'd had rent to pay, work to do, travel to plan. Meanwhile I observed my former high school classmates from afar as they discovered "real" college life. The fraternities. The drinking. The fifteen pounds they packed on during their freshman year.

Truthfully those things were attractive during my senior year in high school. In retrospect I understood why; I needed a break from running at full speed for too long. I watched from afar as former classmates adopted that lifestyle—and crashed. Besides my passing out in DC, my gap year saved me from having to learn the consequences of those habits personally.

Now I knew who I was regardless of the situation, the country, or the people around me. I was "cool" for having traveled so much and following my own path, a designation that didn't require alcohol or exclusive party invites to achieve.

"So what year are you?" the Brooks Brothers-shirt-donning boy next to me asked on the first day of class.

Finding a quick answer to that question was an unfortunate drawback of my gap years. I had a hard time fitting myself into a box. Since I'd completed my first semester of freshman year while abroad, I had the credits of a freshman but the age of a junior. I didn't really know who to hang out with. Most of the time, I felt I had more in common with graduate students.

The PowerPoint presentation behind a historic oak desk clicked on, and my professor began to ask questions. "Can anyone tell me a consequence of what bringing this bill to the floor now would be?" The room was silent.

I raised my hand. "Well, given the current political polarization of Congress, I'd recommend writing the essence of the bill as a rider on a less controversial piece of legislation. That way representatives on the other side of the aisle who personally agree with the positive impacts of the bill—but can't outright support it for fear of party isolation—wouldn't have to risk their voting record in the name of social betterment."

The timeworn professor removed his bifocals. "That's an interesting approach. Could you please tell the class where in the textbook you learned such a maneuver?"

"I uh…I learned it from life."

My internships taught me what the textbooks don't say. On the other hand, they highlighted the gaps in my understanding, inspiring me to fill them in with classes. Instead of pacing and pondering over my class schedule, I could now take one look at a syllabus and know whether to enroll or save the cash.

The "reverse" approach of "life learning before college learning" reignited my craving for school, taught me how other cultures solve problems, and gave me time to recognize the value of an education.

Those two years also taught me personal finance. They saved me some $200,000 on a degree for a job I now know I wasn't cut out for—four degrees, if I count all the times I got an internship and realized I didn't want to pursue that major. In total those two years cost me less than two semesters at my local state school. I knew how to support myself financially through paid internships, savings, and scholarships. To save more I could have taken fewer projects or stayed closer to home.

The Brooks Brothers boy leaned over to me again. "You know, you've got a lot of time, but have you ever considered declaring government as your major?" He delivered the lines with an honest, helpful voice.

I smiled. I'd known my role on campus and my academic purpose at college the moment I'd touched down in Boston. I'd been elected vice president of the Harvard Extension Student Association while living in DC, and my professional experience had helped me determine my major (government), minor (two, actually—Mandarin Chinese and general management), and career path (management consulting).

I didn't feel a need to count down the days to the moment when I would declare my major or when I would graduate. My two gap years taught me that life is lived every day, not just on the days that I think will bring me happiness. I wish I'd learned that earlier! How much better high school would have been if I'd lived each day individually instead of waiting for the fateful one that brought me the envelopes I resealed with my tears.

When class ended, I walked admiringly through the famed gates of Harvard Yard, now framed in ivy leaves of autumn amber, caramel, and gold. Taking a gap year before college isn't a guarantee that you'll get into better schools than you might have before you left. However, I hope my story shows that doing so can be an advantage in the eyes of admissions committees and corporations. Certainly, my two years off revealed the importance of choosing a school that meets your standards for selection, not just the other way around.

Taking a year off isn't right for everyone. It's not just for the world's heiresses, the indecisive, or quitters either. It's for you and me—those of us who are looking for a new path to higher education. Those of us who listen to our hearts instead of society. Those of us who want to discover through real-life experience what we love before committing our futures to it.

Now that my gap years have come to a close, I wish I could send the admissions committees that rejected me in 2010 a letter. This time, with two words—thank you.

Now what? It's time to find *your* answer.

ABOUT THE AUTHOR

Monika Lutz redefined the gap year to include professional, academic, and personal pursuits in addition to travel. She is passionate about sharing her internship and travel experiences with students and encouraging them to pursue their unique ambitions before following the beaten path. Monika is currently working towards an undergraduate degree in government with a double minor in Mandarin Chinese and general management from Harvard University Extension School where she is the first female vice president of The Harvard Extension Student Association (HESA) and an elected board member of the prestigious Harvard Cooperative Society.

Monika attended high school in Boulder, Colorado where she was the Head Girl (student body co-president), a varsity lacrosse player, a National Honor Society club executive, and earned her International Baccalaureate Degree with a perfect score in economics. Monika has been featured in *The Wall Street Journal*, *Time*, *Fox News*, and *Glamour.* Her own writing has been published in *USA Today*, *The Colorado Daily*, *Pink Pangea* and many more.

ADDITIONAL RESOURCES

For students who are interested in interning in China, below is the contact information for the company that made some of the experiences described here possible.

Next Step Connections
Web: www.nextstepconnections.com
Email: contact@nextstepconnections.com
China Office Phone Number: +86 (21) 6322 5990

Facebook: www.facebook.com/nextstepconnections
Twitter: twitter.com/NSCinternship
Youtube: www.youtube.com/user/NextStepConnections
Linkedin: www.linkedin.com/company/next-step-connections-ltd

CPSIA information can be obtained
at www.ICGtesting.com
Printed in the USA
LVOW10s0001300318
571738LV00009B/355/P